The Church: Paradox and Mystery

alba house. DIVISION OF THE SOCIETY OF ST. PAUL
STATEN ISLAND, N. Y. 10314

Henri de Lubac, S.J.

The Church:
Paradox and Mystery

Translated from the French by
James R. Dunne

Originally published under the title *Paradoxe et Mystère de l'Église,* © 1967 Editions Montaigne, Paris.

This edition © 1969 Ecclesia Press

Nihil Obstat: Patrick J Hamell DD

Imprimatur: ✠ Michael A Harty DD
Ennis, 28 August 1969

Library of Congress Catalog Card Number: 75-110784

SBN: 8189-0175-6

This book was printed, bound and published by the Priests and Brothers of the Society of St. Paul, 2187 Victory Blvd., Staten Island, N.Y. as a part of their communications apostolate.

CONTENTS

PREFACE

Each of the seven chapters of this book is a marginal gloss on the Second Vatican Council, more precisely, on the Constitution *Lumen Gentium*. (I am writing elsewhere on the Constitutions *Dei Verbum* and *Gaudium et Spes*.) Their unity primarily derives from this fact. They partake moreover of a common inspiration or, if one prefers, a common concern. None of them pretends to sketch the results of new critical researches or to tackle head on the serious doctrinal problems that for some time now have been presenting themselves ever more acutely to the consciences of believers. Neither does any of them treat explicitly the complex and delicate tasks that confront us on the road of renewal which the entire Church has taken. While I have permitted myself to venture, here and there, an opinion on one or another of today's controversial questions, I have sought to avoid strict topicality.

The *object* of this little book is nonetheless topical. Owing to the diverse occasions that gave rise to them, the different chapters are composed in different styles but, for all that, tend to a single end: as I recalled them to myself, I have tried to make some very simple truths stand out; truths that, for the most part, are linked to the very foundations of Christian faith and life, and which one would like to be able to say are held in common. What, in other circumstances, might appear banal and conformist will today, perhaps, appear in another light . . . I have every confidence that those who are sincerely working for renewal in the Church, even if they repudiate such or such an opinion put forward in this book, will understand and approve the spirit which led me to set it down.

The first chapter is a mediation read at a Bible vigil in the course of the Notre Dame Theological Congress in March 1966 (South Bend, Indiana). Chapters two and three are developments of papers read at the above-mentioned congress and also a similar congress in Rome in September 1966. The fourth has appeared in an abbreviated form in the *Bulletin du cercle Saint–Jean–Baptiste* (September 1966). The last three chapters appeared as articles in, respectively, *Christus* (December 1964), *Civitas* (Lucerne, July 1965) and *Recherches et debats* (September 1966).

From Paradox
to Mystery

In his journeying through this world the Christian periodically asks himself, 'what is the Church?' It may seem to him no bad thing—particularly if he is a theologian—to set aside for a time critical studies, sociological analyses, exegetical treatises, symposia, theories, in short, all the diverse shapes and forms which a reasoning, cerebral theology may take. Relaxed, he now puts his question again, but contemplatively, closer to the spirit of an old and venerable tradition that termed precisely this activity 'theology'. Indeed such an attitude may appear not only good but necessary if it is true that the alpha and omega of the great question he has posed is summed up in the single word, mystery. *De Ecclesiae mysterio*: such, as we know, is the title given to the first chapter of the recent conciliar Constitution, *Lumen Gentium*. To approach the mystery, however, let us first tackle a more modest reality, the paradox of the Church.

(The language and underlying sensibility of this meditation will appear foreign to many of our non-Catholic brethren. Should they happen to read it, I will ask them to bear patiently with what is a simple witness.)

What a paradox indeed this Church of ours presents! How real a paradox! What a wealth of contrasting aspects her history offers, each refusing to be neatly catalogued! Soon to reach her two-thousandth birthday she can look behind her to such a succession of changes, developments, crises, metamorphoses. And even today, in a world tending more and more to uniformity, how great the distance—and sometimes the abyss—that separates Christian communities in different countries in their mentalities, their ways of living and thinking about the faith (not to speak of the ruptures caused by schism). Moreover, have we not found individuals and groups, at the same time and in the same place, declaring their utter devotion and allegiance to the Church and, with equal energy, their almost total opposition to one another? Little wonder that an acute observer was recently moved to remark that professing Catholicism, far from being a principle of unity, was much more likely to be one of division.

The Church . . . I begin my personal search, but where shall I find her? What are the features of her countenance? With all these disparate elements, can she in fact be said to have a countenance? I believe so; she is *complexio oppositorum*. But even so, at first sight I must surely admit that the resounding clash of the *opposita* hides the unity of the *complexio*. Or is this merely the inevitable result of regarding her successively from different points of view? Or is the truth of the matter that she embraces each of the incompatibles? I am told that she is holy, yet I see her full of sinners. I am told of her mission to raise man above earthly cares, to remind him of his heavenly vocation, yet I see her endlessly busy with the temporal things of this earth, almost as if she wished to instal us permanently here. I am assured that she is universal, as open as intelligence or divine charity, yet so often her members, as if under some compulsion, huddle together in closed enclaves, just like human beings everywhere. She is called immutable, the reliable lynch-pin in the chaos of history, and yet look now!—under our very eyes, the rapidity of her renewal in our time alarms many of her own members.

Yes, a paradox is this Church of ours! I have played no cheap rhetorical trick. A paradox of a Church for paradoxical mankind and one that on occasion adapts only too much to the exigencies of the latter! She espouses its characteristics with all the attendant complexities and illogicalities—with the endless contradictions that are in man. We see this in every age, and the critics and the pamphleteers—a proliferating breed, alas—have a joyous time of it, rubbing it all in. Since the early days, indeed while she was taking the first halting steps outside the confines of Jerusalem, the Church was reflecting the traits—the miseries —of mankind.

But we must focus our attention a little more carefully and bypass the quantitative illusion that always hides the essential. The essential is never perceived in sheer multiplicity or in first impressions. In this way we shall perceive the paradox proper to the Church and it is this paradox which will introduce us to the mystery.

The Church is at once human and divine, at once a gift from

above and a product of this earth. She is composed of men each of whom resists with all the weight of a laggard and wounded nature the life the Church strives to infuse. She is orientated towards the past, which contains a memorial she well knows is never past; she tends towards the future, elated by the hope of an ineffable consummation of whose nature no sensible sign gives a hint. Destined in her present form to leave all behind as 'the image of this world', she is destined in her innermost nature to remain intact for the day when what she is will be manifested. Multiple or multiform, she is nonetheless *one,* of a most active and demanding unity. She is a people, the great anonymous crowd and still—there is no other word—the most personal of beings. Catholic, that is, universal, she wishes her members to be open to everything and yet she herself is never fully open but when she is withdrawn into the intimacy of her interior life and in the silence of adoration. She is humble and she is majestic. She professes a capacity to absorb every culture, to raise up their highest values; at the same time we see her claim for her own the homes and hearts of the poor, the undistinguished, the simple and destitute masses. Not for an instant does she cease—and her immortality assures continuity—to contemplate him who is at once crucified and resurrected, the man of sorrows and lord of glory, vanquished by, but saviour of, the world. He is her bloodied spouse and her triumphant master. From his generous heart, ever open and yet always infinitely secret, she has received her existence and the life it is her wish to communicate to all.

How to perceive and grasp her real nature, this is still my question. The harder I try to see, the more I am forced to abandon my false analogies; I am dazzled by her profound truth—and I give up in despair any attempt to define her. And even if I then ask her to define herself, her answer is a rich profusion of biblical images which I well understand are not mere teaching aids but so many allusions to a reality, in its essence always beyond the reach of my natural intelligence. Yes, even after the splendid achievement of logical, clear exposition that is *Lumen Gentium,* her most lucid self-definition yet, my meditation is still in the cul-de-sac of mystery.

And yet I do have something to show for my pains, something obvious, literally childlike; something I knew before I

3

began and which every reflection confirmed. I can tell it in one word, the first of all words: the Church is my mother. Yes, the Church, the whole Church, that of generations past who transmitted her life, her teachings, her witness, her culture, her love to me; and the Church of today. The whole Church, I say, not only the institutional Church, or the Church teaching, or, as we still say, the hierarchical Church that holds the keys confided to her by the Lord. No, more broadly and simply, I mean the 'living Church', working, praying, active and contemplative, remembering and searching, believing, hoping, loving; the daily forger of innumerable links, visible and invisible, between her members; the Church of the humble, close to God; this 'secret army', recruiting from every quarter, braving the periods of decadence, loyal and self-sacrificing, without thought of revolt or even reform, always taking the road that ascends despite a fallen nature that beckons elsewhere, testifying in silence to the continuing fecundity of the gospel and to the already present kingdom. Much more, the entire Church, without distinction, that immense flock of Christians, so many of whom are unaware of their royal priesthood and of the fraternal community they constitute, all this is my mother too.

In this community I find my support, my strength and my joy. It was here that I first met the Church, at the knees of my earthly mother, and ever since it is here I still best recognize her through the mist of mere events and situations that in the long run defy analysis. Her experience, she tells me, has been the means, down the centuries, of increasing her perception of the sacred truth revealed to her. I too can tell her that my experience, modest and restricted though it be, has allowed me—as it has each of her faithful—to perceive precisely this, that she is my mother. This word which, as I say, is the first, pre-eminently the child's word, is also the word that best resumes whatever perception the adult achieves into the nature of man himself.

The Church is my mother because she brought me forth to a new life. She is my mother because her concern for me never slackens, any more than do her efforts to deepen that life in me, however unenthusiastic my co-operation. And though in me this life may be a fragile and timid growth, I have seen its full flowering in others. I have seen it. I have touched it. I can, and will, vouch categorically for it. I am not deaf to the reproaches

4

directed against my mother (truth to tell there are times when I am deafened by them), nor do I fail to see the justice of some of them. But I assert that before the evidence I have just presented all of them—and any others you care to add—are without force and will always remain so. Just as the Church is entirely concentrated in the Eucharist, it may also be said to be entirely concentrated in a saint. For here is the wonder of it: if my eyes had not always been aware of it, I would not have known what to look at. I would not have known how to see this beauty most rare, most improbable, most disconcerting (because, at first sight, so wholly beyond imagining). What I saw was not the highest imaginable accomplishment of human perfection, nor was it consummate wisdom, but a strange and supernatural beauty opening unknown vistas to me, quite devastating and at the same time answering to some hitherto hidden call. It was a kind of beauty that even if its radiance had shone through but one human being it would have created a bias in favour of its divine source. In a saint, I saw the whole Church pass. *Anima ecclesiastica* were the words chosen centuries ago to describe the phenomenon—both words untranslatable today through over-use, but to whose reality the history of the Church testifies many times over. A reality, too, present in our own generation.

Happy those who from childhood have learnt to look on the Church as a mother! Happier still those whose experience, in whatever walk of life, has confirmed its truth! Happy those who one day were gripped by (and whose appreciation of it ever grew) the astonishing newness, richness and depth of the life communicated to them by this mother!

This newness I speak of is a phrase of St. Irenaeus who uses it when speaking of Jesus Christ: *omnem novitatem attulit, semetipsum afferens.*[1] This richness is the promise of salvation in Christ, the news of which St. Paul said he had received the mission to announce to all men (Eph 2:7; cf. 1:18). The depth is that revealed to us by the Spirit of Christ, he who searches the depths of God (1 Cor 1:10). In a word, the Church is our mother because she gives us Christ. She brings about the birth of Christ in us. She says to us, as Paul did to his beloved Corinthians: *In Christo Jesu per Evangelium vos genui.* In her maternal function

---

1. *Adversus haereses*, bk 4, c. 34, n. 1.

she is the spouse, 'glorious and without blemish', which the Man-God brought forth from his pierced heart to unite himself with her 'in the ecstasy of the cross' and to make her fruitful for all time. (And this is the reason, as one of the principal speakers at the Council pointed out,[2] why the mystery of the Church will always be linked with that of the cross.)

Once this is seen—though 'seen' is not quite the word—all further need to exorcise the appearances goes. One may contemplate and love the Church as a mother. Also gone is the need to have preserved the freshness and simplicity of the early ages. Today, yes even today, the Church gives us Jesus. She explains him, shows us how to see him, keeps his presence alive for us.[3]

That much said, what more remains? What would I know of him without her; what would bind me to him, if she did not? Even those who scarcely know her or misunderstand her, do they realize that if they still receive Christ it is to the Church they owe it? 'Who will separate us from the charity of Christ? Who will separate us from the love of God which is in Christ Jesus?' Paul well knew that no created force could do so. Still, a living link, a new Jacob's ladder, is needed to ensure his passage down the centuries to us. 'For millions upon millions of believers (found in the most alert societies) Christ, since his first appearance, has inexorably reasserted with ever greater vigour his urgent and all-pervading presence',[4] and we do, in fact, firmly endorse St. Paul's belief that no crisis will ever separate us from him.

But make no mistake about it, we owe this confidence to the Church. Jesus lives for us. But without the visible continuity of the Church, the desert sands would have long since swallowed up, if not perhaps his name and memory, certainly the influence of his gospel and faith in his divinity. Had the first Christian community not created, in the fervour of its faith and love, an

2. Cardinal Döpfner, 4 December 1962: 'The mystery of the cross is always at the heart of the Church'.

3. 'Just as a mother explains to her child what the world is, what there is in it to be seen, how to look at it, etc., so the Church, taking her cue from the mother of the Lord, the believer par excellence, teaches her children the word of God; she transmits, thanks to her dual experience of being both mother and spouse, not simply the sense but the taste and flavour, the concrete and incarnated character of this word' (Hans Urs von Balthasar, La Gloire et la Croix, vol. 1).

4. Teilhard de Chardin.

environment sensitive to the Spirit who raised up the evangelists; if, from generation to generation, the Christian communities had not maintained themselves substantially similar to the first, handing on the cult of their Lord; if, as the necessity arose, learned churchmen or courageous leaders or humble witnesses had not championed the purity and integrity of inalterable dogma (as Pope Zephyrinus in the third century, though with no head for metaphysics and caught between the exquisite subtleties of the learned—and contradictory—proposals of Hippolytus and Noetus); if the great councils had not for all time determined christological orthodoxy; if there had been a faltering—what would Christ be for us today? 'Without the Church, Christ evaporates or is fragmented or cancels himself out'.[5] And without Christ what would man be?[6]

Whether humanity knows it or not, it needs Christ. Emerging with difficulty from the cosmos that gave it birth, the human spirit, an irreversible force, needs the irreversible victory of Christ to achieve its divine destiny. His mystical body must be the incarnation of humanity, thus allowing humanity to enter into God. Humanity has been adopted by the Father in the person of Jesus, the Son. Its purification and transfiguration must be accomplished by modelling itself on him and receiving his life. It must 'take the form of Christ'. Such is God's design, this mystery hidden to the ancient peoples but revealed to us 'in the fullness of time' by the Son who was with the Father.

This design is to be realized by and in the bosom of the Church. The Spirit of Christ has reposed in her a 'unique power of divinization'. She is the sacrament of Christ, the channel through which the light and the strength of the gospel is communicated to us. In our time she is the axis round which the great mystical

5. Teilhard de Chardin.

6. How true the following, from the pen of Dietrich Bonhoeffer: 'What is important when all is said and done is not what this or that churchman wants; all that need concern us is what Jesus wants'. And again, 'too often we place obstacles before the word of God . . . when we preach our personal convictions and opinions, day in day out, and have little time left over to preach Jesus himself . . . We must search to understand the immensity and richness of what is given us in Christ and discard the essential poverty and narrowness of our personal views and convictions . . . It is only in a commitment without reservation to the demand of Jesus Christ for total obedience that the utter liberation is achieved that is the essential requisite for communion with him' (*The Prize of Grace, the Sermon on the Mount*). Experience moreover shows us that as the connection with the Church is lessened, so the face of Jesus begins to recede.

re-assembly must group itself. The Hebrew Jerusalem was no more than the weak capital of a tiny nation, continually at the mercy of the powerful empires surrounding her. Indeed, the Church, the new Jerusalem, may seem to us today equally small and weak, her faith shaken, her resources derisory, her very witness barely evident. Powerful forces have assailed her, with the steel fist or the velvet glove according to the spirit of the time, forces of the flesh and forces of the mind. And sometimes their success seemed assured: she was silenced, undermined, fragmented. She is the spiritual heiress of old Jerusalem indeed, but also 'the privileged, central Axis', 'the Axis of progress and assimilation', 'the vibrant Axis of life';[7] round her at the end will gather every being destined for transformation, salvation and eternal life. The psalmist's prophecy applies to her:

> Glorious things are said of you,
> O City of God!
> I will list Rahab and Babylon among my admirers;
> And the Philistines,
> The inhabitants of Tyre and Ethiopia,
> It was there that they were born!
> They all call Sion 'my mother'!
> Each one of them was born in her,
> And it was the Most High himself who founded her!
> Jahweh writes in the register of the peoples:
> It was there that they were born!
>
> (Psalm 86:3–6)

As our humanity grows it transforms itself; the Church must not lag behind in achieving its own renewal, using to do so its jealously-guarded heritage. But her rapport with Christ remains a constant. Her ability to give birth does not diminish. She does not retire into herself, fearful; on the contrary, she serenely opens welcoming arms, giving her all. And when more than her all seems called for, when the huge demands on her mother-hood threaten to overwhelm her, then she confidently turns to her spouse. She has her problem children: some take fright, some are scandalized; some, losing touch with her Spirit, declare that the time is ripe for a complete overhaul and present, for its

---

7. Teilhard de Chardin, 13 December 1918, etc.

accomplishment, their 'private blueprints—revolutionary or subversive'. At such times it is the duty of all who recognize her as mother to demonstrate their unfaltering attachment and their anxiety, in St. Paul's words, 'to be made new in mind and spirit',[8] that they may thereby accomplish her mission in a patience at once humble and dynamic. Because she carries the hope of the world.

It happens that men, blindly forgetting that all they have they owe to her, leave this holy Church. It happens too, as no one living in our age will deny, that the mother is attacked by those she is still nourishing. A wind of sweeping, mindless criticism is blowing through the Church and has not been unsuccessful in turning heads and alienating affections. It is a sirocco, sterile and hostile to the breath of the Spirit. Contemplating my mother's humiliated face, I will love her only twice as much. Without trading polemic for polemic, I will take pains to show her my love even in her guise of slave. While others allow themselves to be hypnotized by the wrinkles that are only natural to the features of the old, how much more truly will love show me her hidden strength, her silent dynamism—in a word, her perpetual youth—'the mighty forces issuing from her heart, finally ravishing all men's hearts'.[9]

Today she is demanding—as she has rarely done before—a massive effort from all of us to gear ourselves to the reality of an age of change. If we respond seriously the result will surely be her 'new spring'. To accomplish the task it is vital to understand the conditions that will guarantee it. Openness and renewal, these are the key-words of the programme. Both are open to misrepresentation. The openness must derive from strong roots in the essentials, the renewal from personal fidelity. 'Only the authentic Christian is a force for renewal in the world.' It would be sad indeed if, under the pretext of 'openness' and 'renewal' I was to adore, in Newman's phrase, the vague and pretentious creations of my mind instead of the Son ever-living in his Church. Sad, too, if I placed faith in purely human novelties whose life-span is brief and whose disappearance certain; or if I tried to go it alone, fashioning willy-nilly from

8. Eph 4:23.
9. Teilhard de Chardin.

9

the deep wells of truth some private credo, repudiating the offer of infallible wisdom bequeathed by the Spouse to his Betrothed.[10] May God grant my continued understanding of one thing: attachment to the Church's tradition, far from being a stumbling block, is the principle of all effective audacity.[11]

Finally, to deepen my conviction I shall appeal to two witnesses; they will serve me as intercessors.

'We receive the Spirit of God if we love the Church'. So the great St. Augustine tells me. 'We are assembled by charity if we rejoice to bear the name of Catholic and profess the true faith'. Few people have had the genius, the depth of experience and the strong personality of Augustine. Few men, if any, have explored the subjective consciousness as he did, so that for centuries the thinking of the West on the nature of man was shaped by him. On the other hand, few men have suffered as he did or were scandalized as he was by the sight of the Church 'in the guise of a slave'. But individual greatness or individual spiritual gifts—no matter how great—he counted as nothing if they placed obstacles to the gift of God which comes to man through the Church. He knew that 'the freedom-principle in the Church is inseparable from her organized state'.[12] He grew to understand this better and better.

He realized also that no trial, however great, could break the bond of catholic unity. Nor would this unity ever depend on an individual: such a pretentious sacrilege could only come from a 'false lover of the Spouse'. The true 'friend of the Spouse'

---

10. Cf. Newman, 'Sermon on the Humiliation of the Eternal Son'.

11. Cf. Yves Congar OP, 'Changements et continuité dans l'Eglise': 'This Church is essentially a communion: I exist in it as a participant in a common life, deriving from the same head, the same soul, the same principles. This concrete reality, out of space and time, envelops and supports me, gives me life and nourishes my spiritual being. What would I be, what would my faith, my prayer, be if I were given the Bible and thereafter left to my own devices? Indeed, what would be the point in having a Bible at all? I have received everything from and in the Church. Any recompense I might offer is totally inadequate. And the recompense itself? Why it is taken in its entirety from the treasure the Church has already given me. I am only a moment out of an immense life that has been personalized in me (and this aspect is magnificent!) but which includes and surpasses me, which existed before me and which will survive me. I have nothing!' (in *La France Catholique*, March 1967).

12. Teilhard de Chardin, 4 November 1916. Also, in 1935: 'How glad we are of the Church's authority! Left to ourselves there is no extravagance we would not be capable of'. Cf. Mgr. de Solages, *Teilhard de Chardin* (Privat, 1967), p. 341.

takes care to ensure in himself first of all the incorruptibility of the Spouse. What counted, he believed, was not superior knowledge or wisdom, but superior obedience and humility. He never tires of repeating this. For himself, Augustine was content to be a man of the Church, indefatigibly preaching the unity that triumphs over every division and by whose witness love has the last word. For him, as for Irenaeus, 'where the Church is, there is the Spirit of God'. 'In the measure that one loves the Church of Christ', he tells us, 'one possesses the Holy Spirit.' The overriding concern for the Church manifested by such statements will appear limiting only to those who have never understood the universality of the Man-God: 'The Church is the exact limit of the horizon of Christ's redemption, just as, for us, Christ is the horizon of God'.[13]

And from among other churchmen, my fathers in the faith, I choose another intercessor, vastly different from the ingenious Augustine: a man who is still close to us, the man we call 'good Pope John'.[14] Pope John was not what you would call a reformer. Neither was he one for ideologies. He did not despise the past, he was not a compulsive critic. He was a good priest of 'lively and simple' faith, his way of life was traditional, his piety very much in the classic mould. He liked to recall his models, 'those great and good old priests of Bergamo whose memory is blessed'. He read and enjoyed the *Imitation of Christ* and the *Moralia* of St. Gregory. He loved the Virgin Mary, meditating with her as he recited the rosary. Retreats and a prudent asceticism preserved and nourished his natural tendency 'to an intimate union with God'.

Liberally disposed towards all developments 'that left the sacred deposit of the faith intact' and did not flaunt 'the genuine sentiment of the Church', he abhorred 'pretentious searching for individualist affirmations' and he kept himself on guard against 'the mortal enemy that corrupts all we do'. Love for and fidelity to the Church were his ruling passions as we know from his *Journal of a Soul*—a book of great charm—published

13. Hans Urs von Balthasar, *Introduction à saint Augustin, Le visage de l'Eglise* (Ed. du Cerf, Paris, 1959). Even the election of Israel had given rise to the 'scandal of particularism'.

14. Cf. Georges Chantraine SJ, 'Optimisme, angoisse et espérance chez Jean XXIII' in *Nouvelle revue théologique*, 1964, pp. 369-87.

after his death.[15] This was the man who, 'by a sudden impulse' at a decisive moment in the Church's history, steered Peter's bark 'towards new ways of feeling, wishing and acting'. But even then good Pope John did not become self-important; he remained his good-natured, steady self. With his motto 'obedience and peace'[16] he still voyaged in 'the calm and tranquil sea of the will of God'. His request of all he met was that they should daily implore that, like Jesus, he would be 'sweet and humble of heart'. But as if summoned by his fidelity, the Spirit one day descended on this humble existence—the true Spirit of God, the sole inspirer of true renewal. A prophetic breath stirred a sleeping Church. Its influence spread beyond the Church and at the same time that the good Pope 'found, without having looked for it, the way to modern man's heart', all men had proof, once again, that *the Church lives*.

15. 'The *Journal of a Soul* has a vital message: we can only rejoin modern man, as Christians and apostles, when we have rediscovered certain of the most elementary concepts of Christian asceticism, humanity, sweetness, surrender. The words recur on every page . . .' V. Walgrave OP, *Essai d'autocritique d'un ordre religieux* (Brussels, 1966), pp. 147–8.

16. Cf. Wolfgang Seibel SJ, '"Gehorsam und Friede", Gestalt und Werk Johannes XXIII' in *Geist und Leben,* 1963, pp. 246–70. André Manaranche SJ, *L'homme dans son univers* (Ed. Ouvrières, Paris, 1966), p. 11: 'All dynamism is a product of the interior life. In John XXIII we see once again that the word of God, sown in silence on the fertile ground of a believing heart, is capable of producing a growth of world-shattering importance spreading out from the entire Church. The limpid well that is the man of faith can pour its living water over history (Jn 7:37) and the word whispered in the ear is proclaimed loudly from the roof-tops (Matt 10:27)'.

2

How is the Church
a Mystery?

The Church is a mystery, or in the words of Pope Paul at the opening of the Council's second session, 'a reality impregnated by the presence of God and of a nature, consequently, that permits a constant self-exploring'.[1] And in carrying out this exploration, Pope Paul tells us again in his encyclical *Ecclesiam Suam* that the experience of the faithful soul is more important than pure theology: mystery, of its nature, is not susceptible to the logical processes of the latter, the mystery must be a lived reality.[2]

To begin with, let us attempt some rapid sketches of the notion of mystery, avoiding rational generalizations (a methodological vice that the Constitution *Die Verbum,* speaking in the context of revelation, has tried to free us of)[3] but basing ourselves on what has been, or is believed to have been, revealed.

First, the mystery is somehow linked to God's design for man, whether as marking the limit of or the means of realizing this destiny. It is not, therefore, something irrational or absurd or merely non-contradictory; but, even so, the intellectual approach will always be fruitless. We are dealing with something that defies analysis, a smooth partition-wall, as it were, that one can hurl oneself against but not get a grip on. Neither is it a truth which would remain provisionally out of reach but as human reason attained 'adulthood' would become progressively

1. Speech at the opening of the second session, 29 September 1963 (AAS 55, 1963, p. 848).

2. *Ecclesiam Suam* (AAS 56, 1964, pp. 623–4): 'As we know, this is a mystery, the mystery of the Church . . . it is not a truth restricted to the realms of theological science, it is something to be lived, so that even before the Christian comes to understand it clearly he will already have experienced it intuitively'.

3. *Dei Verbum,* ch. 1. Louis Bouyer has also alluded to this dangerous approach apropos the Eucharist: *Eucharistie* (Desclée, Paris–Tournai, 1966); certain theological positions derive less from texts than from 'a priori concepts of sign and sacrifice'. The eucharistic mystery is scrutinized 'either in the light of what one might call a prefabricated philosophy or a totally irrelevant comparison drawn from the history of comparative religion' (pp. 12 and 14).

more accessible, as man narrowed down the mystery to manageable proportions, a theory held by Leibniz and, more strongly, by Lessing and Herder.[4] The Church is a mystery for all time out of man's grasp because, qualitatively, it is totally removed from all other objects of man's knowledge that might be mentioned. And yet, at the same time, it concerns us, touches us, acts in us, reveals us to ourselves. To this end, it must have a tangible aspect, the incarnated Word of God, expression of the Inexpressible, the efficacious sign to realize the plan of salvation.[5]

The visible revelation par excellence of mystery is, therefore, the life of Christ. This was the inspiration of our brief and still abstract description so far. The actions of Christ are genuinely human actions, set in history; but being also the acts of a divine Person, in each of them God becomes humanly visible and tangible. To understand the meaning of Christ's life is to penetrate into the divine reality. 'What do you mean, "show us the Father"? Philip, he who sees me sees the Father' (John 14:9). By and in Christ God has become for us, in the sense I have just used, a mystery; not the inaccessible boundary that reason forces us to impose, or at the opposite spectrum, the object of reason's possible construction and, consequently, reason's eventual mastery. No, in Christ God has become the Being who in his inner life as in his free designs has consented to become an object of our knowledge. And, try as we may, it is a subject we shall never exhaust.

I

'The epiphanic Word of God',[6] manifestation of his being and of his salvific design, Christ is not only *a* mystery: he is *the* mystery—there is no other. When St. Paul speaks of the mystery of Christ he understands the term as wholly encompassing the object of divine revelation. So, too, St. John of the Cross when, following the Epistle to the Hebrews, he explains that in giving

4. Cf. Kant, 'Answer to the Question: What is Revelation?': '. . . The minority is incapable of making use of its insights except under the direction of some other person . . . *Sapere aude*; have the courage to act on your own insight!'

5. Our source here is Yves de Montcheuil sj, *Problèmes de vie spirituelle* (Ed. de l'Epi, Paris, 7th ed., 1959), pp. 185–92.

6. René Latourelle, sj, 'Le Christ Signe de la révélation selon la constitution *Dei Verbum*' in *Gregorianum*, 47, 1966, p. 698.

us his Son, his unique Word, God has given us everything and has said all.[7] And, again, as St. Augustine neatly puts it: *Non est aliud Dei mysterium, nisi Christus.*[8]

The Church is, therefore, a mystery; but a mystery must derive from something. The Church is a mystery because, coming from God and entirely at the service of his plan, she is an organism of salvation, precisely because she relates wholly to Christ and apart from him has no existence, value or efficacity.

In the opening passage of his first encyclical, *Ecclesiam Suam,* Pope Paul gave voice to the same idea; and again, in words that impressed all who heard him, during his discourse at the opening of the second session of the Council: 'Let no other light shine in this assembly but Christ, the light of the world; let no truth dwell in our hearts but the truth we find in the words of Christ, our only Master . . .' In the same speech he referred to the mosaic in St. Paul's Outside the Walls which depicts Pope Honorius III, symbolizing the entire Church, prostrate before the Pantocrator; Pope Paul dramatically demonstrated all he had said by going himself to worship in the Holy Places.[9]

In an allocution of 23 November 1966, he said again: 'Relate her wholly to Christ, her real architect and builder, and you will understand the Church'.[10] No different is the teaching of the Council whose historic Constitution on the Church opens with the words, *'Lumen gentium cum sit Christus . . .'* A simple and evident truth; so simple and evident indeed that its explicit statement might seem redundant at a learned congress of theologians or in a document destined to be read by all Catholics, however poorly instructed. And yet this is a truth so beneficial that every possible occasion should be seized to meditate it; a truth so illuminating that the Council's setting it into relief

7. *Ascent of Mount Carmel,* bk 2, ch. 22: '. . . in which the Apostle gives us to understand that God has become, as it were, dumb and has nothing more to say . . . He who would now seek to question him . . . would do God an injury in not resting his glance entirely on Christ . . . God might well say to him: "I have already said all there is to say in my Word, my Son".'

8. *Letter* 187 (to Dardanus), c. 11, n. 34 (PL 33, 845): . . . *in quo oporteat vivificari mortuos in Adam.*

9. Cf. below, ch. 5. Note the contrast between these words of the Pope and another formula, also heard in St. Peter's during the Council: *ad laudem Dei et decus Ecclesiae.*

10. See also Pope John XXIII on the symbolism of the paschal candle: 11 September 1962 (AAS 54, pp. 679-80).

moved a non-Catholic Christian to remark: 'The ecclesiological problem has found its renewal'. Through this concept, so full of promise, and 'taken full cognizance of by the Council, the Church affirms that her understanding of herself will come not so much from her structures or her history as from her predestination in Jesus Christ and her orientation towards the parousia'.[11] To forget this fundamental truth, to allow its slightest neglect, is to court disaster . . .

In this context an old tradition symbolically referred to the mystery of the Church as *Mysterium Lunae*.[12] The Fathers, with incredible ingenuity, drew heavily on this symbol; here we shall remark only its general lines. Christ is the sun of justice, the only source of light. The Church (like the moon) at all times depends on this sun for her brilliance. It is possible, therefore, to speak, with Didymus the Blind, of 'the lunar constitution of the Church'.[13] As the moon shines in the night, so does the Church illumine the darkness of the age and of our ignorance, showing us the way to salvation. For all that, her light, wholly borrowed, has only a limited clarity, *refulgentia subobscura,* in St. Bonaventure's phrase.[14] She dispenses the symbols of a truth whose direct brilliance our eyes cannot yet bear. While the sun remains always in glory, the moon (that is, the Church) continually passes through phases, now waxing, now waning, in proportion to the measure of her growth and her inner fervour; for the vicissitudes of the human condition are always her lot.[15]

11. J. J. von Allmen, 'Remarques sur la Constitution *Lumen Gentium*' in *Irenikon*, 39, 1966, pp. 14–15. Cf. Henri de Lubac, *Méditation sur l'Église*, 2nd ed., 1953, ch. 1, 'L'Église est un mystère', and ch. 6, 'Le Sacrement de Jesus-Christ'. Juan Alfaro SJ, 'Cristo, Sacramento de Dios Padre; la Iglesia, Sacramento de Cristo Glorificado' in *Gregorianum*, 48, 1967, pp. 5–27.

12. Hugo Rahner, 'Mysterium Lunae, Zur Kirchentheologie der Väterzeit' in *Zeitschrift für katholische Theologie*, 1939, pp. 311–49. Further on, the image of the sun and the moon is rather awkwardly applied to the relationship between spiritual and temporal powers.

13. *In psalm*. 71, 5 (PG 39, 1465–8).

14. *In Hexaemeron*, collatio 20, n. 13: *Comparatur autem Ecclesia militans lunae, propter refulgentiam subobscuram sive symbolicam—propter refulgentiam excessivam sive extaticam— et propter refulgentiam ordinatam* (ed. Quaracchi, vol. 5, p. 427).

15. Thus St. Thomas Aquinas (*Opera omnia*, Parma, 1863, vol. 14, p. 377): *. . . sive pulchra ut Luna, in praesenti vita, ubi aliquando concessa sibi pace securitate crescit, aliquando adversitatibus obscurata decrescit.*

But never is the waning so extreme as to cause her total loss; sooner or later she becomes full again.[16] At certain times her witness may falter, the salt of the earth may lose its savour, the 'too human' may get the upper hand, the faith waver in many hearts—but we have the assurance that 'saints will always spring up'.[17]

Let us see if we cannot, with the help of an Origen and an Ambrose, understand the meaning—the real meaning—of the moon's waning. It signifies to us that in this century the Church in the throes of death is finding in its onset the means of her renewal, her drawing ever closer to Christ, her spouse. She then becomes so identified with him that she is, as it were, blotted out by his brilliance. So close to her sun, the crucified Lord, the obscurity of the Passion is her road also to fresh vigour and the attainment of her true fecundity.[18] She plunges into the darkness only to re-emerge into the secret fullness of the life of the Resurrected. 'Christ emptied her in order to bring her to fullness, even as he had emptied himself in order to bring all men to fullness. Thus does the Moon announce the mystery of Christ.'[19] And the waning, far from being an irreversible decline, is even at the same time a dawning. It foretells the definitive absorption of the moon into the sun, as the verse of the Psalm proclaims: 'In those days will arise justice and abundance of peace unto the transformation of the moon' (*Orietur in diebus ejus justitia et abundantia pacis, donec tollatur luna*). In St. Augustine's commentary, 'transformation' (*tollatur*) means primarily the taking away (*auferatur*) of all that is mortal and imperfect in the Church—but also her final apotheosis, being

16. Thus Cassiodorus, *In psalm.* 103, 19: *Luna significat Ecclesiam quae in temporibus facta est, quando eam minui contingit et crescere; quae tamen sic minuitur, ut semper redeunte integritata reparetur . . .*

17. Charles Péguy.

18. Cf. Origen, *In Numer.*, hom. 23, n. 5 (Baehrens, pp. 217-8); this passage deals with the 'new fangled' feasts which, according to the letter, 'seemed exhibitions of superstition rather than religion'.

19. *Christus exinanivit eam ut repleat, qui etiam se exinanivit ut omnes repleret. Ergo annuntiavit Luna mysterium Christi*: St. Ambrose, *In Hexaemeron*, bk. 4, ch. 8, n. 32 (PL 14, 204bc). Origen, *In Ezechielem*, hom. 9, n. 3 (Baehrens, p. 411). Cf. the article on light ('Licht') by J. Ratzinger in *Handbuch theologischer Grundbegriffe*, ed. H. Fries (Kösel Verlag, Munich).

wholly assumed by and exalted in Christ, a partner in the glory of his resurrection.[20]

II

This lunar symbolism is, of course, only an example. The mystery always transcends our definitions. Insofar as it has been revealed, we may speak with some precision about it. But its revelation does not alter its character of mystery, nor does it change the conditions under which we may exercise our minds on it. It cannot be neatly packaged in a precise concept: our very concepts are bewildered, circumscribed by it. Hence the necessity for analogy, image and symbol. And even these are not without their pitfalls.

To begin with, if an analogy is not always refined anew, it will lead to error. This applies in particular to analogies drawn from the political and social orders that present themselves so spontaneously. They are indispensable since the Church, being a visible society, is involved with government. But such analogies carry a double danger: on the one hand, we forget that they are precisely only that, analogies; and on the other hand they encourage our natural tendency to hammer out the thoughts of God into some shape that approaches our own ideas.

Unnuanced remarks on the monarchical government of the Church in regard to the papacy, for instance, or on the parliamentary system in regard to ecumenical councils have too often gone uncorrected. The deviations describing themselves as 'conciliar' towards the end of the Middle Ages are well known. So, too, is the famous example of Joseph de Maistre's work, *Du Pape* (1819). A book of considerable merit, its ecclesiological views were too much conditioned by the author's political philosophy, and resulted in certain ultramontane excesses in the last century. Rather more than right reason would countenance, de Maistre was persuaded that 'the dogmas and maxims of stringent discipline in the Catholic Church are, for the most

---

20. St. Augustine, *In psalm.* 71, n. 10 (PL 36, 908). The image is recalled again by Olegario Gonzales Hernandez, 'La nouvelle conscience de l'Église' in *L'Église de Vatican II,* vol. 2, 1966, p. 191. St. Bonaventure associated it with another image drawn from the Canticle of Canticles: '. . . then is realized this word: take no heed of my darkened head, it is the sun that has burned me . . .' (*In Hexaemeneron*, 20, 16; Quaracchi, 5, 428).

part, only the *laws of the world* given divine force and sometimes, too, only innate ideas or the venerable traditions sanctioned by revelation'. Small wonder the pope of the time displayed considerable reticence when the author offered to dedicate the work to him.[21] In his treatise *De l' Église et de sa divine constitution*, which has recently appeared in a new edition, Dom Gréa, though still marked by traditionalist thinking, saw fit to recall the necessity of going beyond the method where de Maistre bogged down: 'We are dealing here with a mystery, and reason, basing itself on human parallels, cannot hope to decipher it. Human governments and their executive branches are totally divorced from the mystery that is the Church. Our search must be on a higher plane: we must seek in the august Trinity the reason for and the type of all the Church's life'.[22]

But all of that is in the past and we cannot afford to dwell on it overlong. Rather than to the institution of the papacy or the councils, it is to the fact of collegiality, once more given a place of honour by the Second Vatican Council, that we may fittingly direct our attention. And yet, in the brusque vivacity of its rebirth, the very same risk exists for the collegiality doctrine, namely, that it will conform itself in theory and practice to man-made models. Its force may be whittled away while it searches for means of organizing itself, forgetting (a) that the true, divinely-granted collegiality is marked by concern for the *universal* Church and (b) that its most common action consists not in the exercise of jurisdiction at all but in the active and habitual interest of each bishop in the faith, life and discipline of the Church, the spread of the kingdom of God, and the bishop's realization of his *personal* responsibility for all of this.

That we may foresee and guard against certain deviations in the application of the liturgical reforms, it will also be useful to

21. The fourth chapter of the first book is entitled, 'Analogies from the temporal power'. Cf. the 2nd ed. (1821), vol. I, p. vi. The author thought of adding as an epigraph to his work: 'Too many princes are worth nothing; a single sovereign is what is needed'. Cf. 24th ed., Pélagaud, Lyons, 1876, pp. viii and xx: 'At Rome . . . they were dumbfounded by this new system', etc.

22. *Op. cit.,* ed. of 1885, p. 126. A new edition has appeared, with preface by Louis Bouyer (Castermann, 1965). Dom Gréa shows considerable interest in the 'mystery of the hierarchy' (p. 290). Cf. M. Schepers OP, 'De notione populi Dei' in *Angelicum*, 43, 1966, p. 335: such an analogy (comparing the Church to a 'perfect society') 'may lead to error'; 'its dangers are obvious', etc.

remark on another similar example: this is the analogy of human assemblies whose features certain people will glibly compare with the celebration of the Eucharistic mystery.[23] Another example (for which we are principally indebted to St. Paul) is that of the human body. Using this image, founded on Scripture though it is, one could reach certain conclusions not only erroneous but absurd. The robust good sense of Paul Claudel draws our attention to this while at the same time introducing us to an essential aspect of the mystery which we shall return to later:

> 'Member of the Church' we say. Well and good, so long as we understand that we are speaking in metaphor. A toe is only a toe and has no pretentions to be the whole body. But the body of the Church is not so constructed, by addition: at no time is it lacking in perfection. Just as the body of Christ is in each particle of the Host so the Church—the whole Church—is behind the face of every Christian. When he speaks, the Church speaks and is heard saying *Perfecta mea*. At the moment of the annunciation Mary was already the entire Church . . .[24]

We know, too, how a too material application of this physical image to the members of the Church, an application that arises from 'the absolute and univocal identification of the (mystical) body of Christ with the visible institution founded by him' has led to extreme theories of who exactly does or does not belong to the true Church. The correction or softening of such theses was very much the concern of the Council, especially in the second chapter of *Lumen Gentium*.[25] Some may still remember the discussion on whether the Church was born on Calvary out of the pierced side of Christ, or whether in the cenacle at Pentecost. A rather sterile point, you may think, yet for a time it set certain theologians very severely at odds with one another. No doubt the disagreement had profound theological roots but, as it stands, the question does not allow of an answer.

23. *Lumen Gentium*, n. 22 and 23. Cf. the observations of J. Ratzinger and J.–C. de Groot in *L'Église de Vatican II*, vol. 3, pp. 774-5 and 825-8. Cf. my *Méditation sur l'Église* (3rd ed., Aubier, Paris, 1954), pp. 131–2; and *Corpus mysticum* (2nd ed., 1949), pp. 293–4.

24. *Emmaüs* (1949), pp. 141–2.

25. Cf. Christopher Butler, 'Les chrétiens non catholiques et l'Église' in *L'Église de Vatican II*, vol. 2, 1966, p. 663.

The effort to determine a day of birth for the Church indicates a tendency to equate her with either a human being or an exterior and artificial society. The authentic tradition suffered no such embarrassment: the texts which have come down to us mention both, without seeing in it either dilemma or contradiction.[26] The Church is both 'the sacred fruit of the tree of the cross' and 'the gift made to the world by the Holy Spirit'; neither excludes the other.

Even with scriptural warrant and due correction an image or analogy is always inadequate. All it ever does is portray an aspect—of greater or lesser importance—of the mystery and even when freed from error by refinement still does not penetrate to the integral truth. An image is practicable, but even when duly purged of inadequacies its best function is to complete another image—or images.[27] Here, too, revelation is our guide. In describing the Church for us it adds image to image, and Christian tradition has meditated the mystery of the Church by commentary on them.

The Church is the ark that saves us from death, as the ark of Noah saved him from the flood—this ark where are found, as the Anglican theologian George Horne would put it, 'the happy days of Eden'. But we are not mere passengers in this ark: we *are* the ark, we are the Church. And so she must be also said to be a people, an assembly. Not that she is the *result* of our assembly; one becomes a Christian only through her. She is therefore a mother, she brings us forth to life in Christ. But this mother keeps us always in her womb and her union with her spouse is so intimate that she is his body and we, consequently, become his members. She is the 'house of faith' into which we

---

26. See, for example, St. Augustine, *In Johannem,* tract. 120, n. 1: 'This second Adam bowed his head and fell asleep on the cross so that a spouse might be formed for him from his side as he slept' (CCL 36, 661). And Pius XI: 'Whoever is moved by the Spirit of God has, spontaneously, the same attitudes, exterior and interior, of the Church, this sacred fruit of the tree of the cross, this gift to an aimless world of the Spirit of God at Pentecost'. Cf. Paul VI, Pentecost homily, 1964 (AAS 56, p. 429); *Doc. cath.,* 61, 1964, col. 695; the encyclical *Ecclesiam suam* (AAS 56, p. 616). Pierre Benoit, *Passion et resurrection du Seigneur* (Paris 1966), p. 219.

27. Cf. Otto Semmelroth SJ, 'L'Église, noveau peuple de Dieu' in *L'Église de Vatican II,* vol. 2, p. 401: 'One cannot completely enclose the nature and proper character of the Church in a single concept or a single image. This conclusion was firmly ratified by the Council . . . Theology is invited to recognize its limits in the effort to grasp the "mystery of the Church".'

must enter to become faithful disciples of Christ. In her is offered the worship pleasing to God; so we call her, too, a temple, or a holy city built of living stone. The term of a long preparation that began with time itself and whose most important stage was the choice of a people to announce her, but at the same time the fruit of the great renewal wrought by Jesus, she is the New Israel.

We are to see in this profusion of imagery, not an incoherent, turbulent or confused growth, nor the mere result of individual and varied study or intuition. Since the images are found in the inspired authors or have been consecrated by tradition, their ultimate source is the Spirit who inspired both. They represent a concurrence to a well-knit unity; not a logical unity, no doubt: he would be a harassed man who attempted to put systematic order on them, or to identify them with one another. From the logical point of view it must be admitted that they are irreducible. If we are to have a sufficient though not exhaustive idea, adequate to our present needs, of what the Church is, all of them are necessary. No one of them gives a clear directive on the attitude God expects of us. We may choose as we please this or that favourite, but none of them can be completely neglected with impunity.

—Yves de Montcheuil[28]

This, in fact, was the line taken by the Council. For many reasons the image of the people of God was given pride of place (in the second chapter of *Lumen Gentium*). To examine into these reasons would be beyond our present scope and would, besides, be incomplete since the inspiration of the Spirit will have to be assigned its role. The following chapters (of the Constitution) are, for the most part, dominated by this image. But the Council, in the first chapter, devoted to the mystery of the Church, recalled at great length first of all a whole series of

28. *Aspects du mystère de l'Église* (Ed. du Cerf, Paris, 1949), pp. 19-22. Cf. Lucien Cerfaux, 'Les images symboliques de l'Église dans le Nouveau Testament' in *L'Église de Vatican II,* vol. 2, pp. 243-58. Giving the Orthodox viewpoint on the Dogmatic Constitution on the Church, Archbishop Basil Krivocheine has written (*Irenikon, 39,* 1966, p. 478): 'One point an Orthodox Christian will be sincerely happy about is that the text does not refer to the "nature" of the Church as the first schema had done, but to its "mystery". This mystery refuses conceptualization but reveals itself in the images of the Church that we find in the Old and New Testaments.'

other images from the Old and New Testaments (n. 6) whose evocative power and analogical richness evidently differ. And, as well, because of its special importance and long-established usage the image of the Body of Christ is then developed in n. 7. So the Council did not forget what it had said earlier: if the image of the people of God was singled out, the others were not forgotten. We may remark also that nowhere in the Constitution is found a definition, strictly speaking, of the people of God from which the whole doctrine might be deduced. If such had happened the result would have been not only the relegating to obscurity of several essential characteristics of the Church but also a sentence of perpetual exile to this obscurity. The Council repudiated such exclusiveness and so, therefore, must we.[29] As Bishop Christopher Butler warns us, 'we must not impose a definition which we then take as an adequate description of the Church'.[30]

III

From the 'mystery' character of the Church we have so far drawn a first consequence: no simple image or concept of the Church wholly succeeds in defining her and the multiplicity of images and concepts offered by Scripture need simultaneous and inclusive treatment, and have been traditionally so treated.

We must now deal with a second consequence. The mystery of the Church, like all mysteries, cannot be taken in with a simple and direct glance but only mirror-like, in our minds. And our minds are confronted with a paradox of a kind that can only be expressed in a series of antithetical, or if you prefer, dialectical sentences. We shall here enumerate three which are not even adequately distinct, all being facets of the same basic paradox: the Church is of God (*de Trinitate*) and she is of men (*ex hominibus*); she is visible and invisible; she is of this earth and this time, and she is eschatological and eternal.

(I) 'In the long run', Newman wrote, 'we shall discover one of two things: either that the Catholic Church is really and effectively the invisible world come to this earth or that our

29. On the Church as the people of God, see the following chapter.

30. *Loc. cit.,* p. 654. Also, Fr. Philipon OP: the Council organized its teaching 'around the notion of the people of God', but 'with great liberty of nuance', etc. (*Points de synthèse de Vatican II,* Ed. Ouvrières, Paris, 1967).

beliefs about our origins and our destiny are sheer fantasy'.[31] The Church is a mysterious extension in time of the Trinity, not only preparing us for the life of unity but bringing about even now our participation in it. She comes from and is full of the Trinity.[32] She is for us—in a favourite phrase of Bossuet— 'Jesus Christ diffused and communicated'. She is 'the Incarnation continued'. She is, as Dietrich Bonhoeffer used to say, 'the presence of Christ on earth, the Christus praesens', she speaks with 'the authority of Christ living and present in her'.[33] By an 'extension of the sense', imposed somehow by virtue of an inner logic, St. Paul applies to her this same word 'mystery' which he had first used of Christ.[34] She is, after all, the spouse of Christ and his body. So perfectly united to him is she that for us 'it is all one' (St. Joan of Arc). She is all-holy and all-sanctifying. As God is our father, she is our mother.

These are not mere *façons de parler*: there is profound truth in all of them. But still, if we were to stop here we would end up in a kind of ecclesiological 'monophysitism' scarcely less false in its one-sidedness—if anything more so—than the christological monophysitism.[35] The fact of the matter is, this Church, this very same Church, is made up of men. She is (or ought to be) wholly subject to Christ; she is a people, often unfaithful and unsubmissive. In her members she is a sinner. The image of the Church as a body is ambivalent, making, as it does, a single organism of Jesus Christ and his Church but signifying at the same time the subjection of the members to the head. The same is true of the image of the moon which we examined earlier: for the Church is also a symbol of perpetual decline and mortality.

31. *Discourses to Mixed Congregations,* p. 282. Cf. Walgrave, *Newman* (1959), p. 218.

32. See my *Méditation sur l'Église,* 2nd ed., pp. 206-7, 325-9.

33. *Gesammelte Schriften,* vol. 1, p. 144, in René Marlé, *Dietrich Bonhoeffer, témoin de Jésus–Christ parmi ses frères* (Castermann, 1967), p. 51.

34. Cf. André Feuillet, *Le Christ Sagesse de Dieu d'après les épîtres pauliniennes* (Gabalda, Paris, 1966), pp. 292-3.

35. Even this of course must be understood analogically, with all the desired nuances, since it is a question precisely of being on guard against an exaggerated assimilation of the Church with Christ. On this, see Yves Congar OP, *Sainte Église* (Ed. du Cerf, Paris, 1964), pp. 69–104; J. N. Nicholas OP, 'Le sens et la valeur en écclésiologie du parallelisme de structure entre le Christ et l'Église' in *Angelicum,* 43, 1966, pp. 353-8: 'Dualism and monophysitism, errors concerning Christ, are, in their fashion, true when applied to the Church' (p. 358). This is exactly what we are trying to show.

If the spiritual side of her illuminates, the carnal obscures; she is ever-changing, *'semper a semetipsa aliena'*, and as persecution reduces her externally, the temptations to which she succumbs ravage her internally.[36] Though her normal duty may be to reflect the light of her sun on men, it may happen that she interposes herself so successfully that an eclipse results; the earth finds itself plunged into darkness.[37] The Church disguises her borrowed splendour in a shabby garment: the contradiction is, therefore, part and parcel of her nature and only the penetrating regard will know how to discover the beauty of her face.[38]

If it is not to be lost sight of, this second, the human, aspect must not—any more than the first—be viewed in isolation. This is the mistake made by certain Protestant ecclesiologies. For these the Church seems to be completely identified with the people of the Old Covenant, the 'stiff-necked' race, invariably repulsing the advances of Yahweh, invariably sinning, invariably deserving of God's anger—and, in the end, invariably receiving his mercy.[39] This one-sidedness again does less than justice to the scriptural texts, taken in their entirety. Notably, it skimps pauline teaching. It fails to take account of and draw the consequences of the Christian novelty. It makes the title *'Ecclesia Mater'*, applied so quickly to the early Church, unintelligible.

Also difficult to see is how it is compatible with the idea of the Church as sacrament, which is sometimes applied to her. Our basic reproach is that it is inspired more by the Old than the New Testament or, in other words, does not enter fully into the logic of the mystery of the incarnation. Karl Barth has the same quarrel with it, observing that under the Old Covenant

36. St. Augustine, *In psalm.* 10, n. 3 (PL 36, 131–3); *Epist.* 55, c. 6, n. 10: 'In her time of pilgrimage, the Church seems obscured as she labours in much wickedness' (PL 33, 209). St. Maximus of Turin, *Hom.* 101 (PL 57, 485–90). Origen, *In I Reg.,* hom. 1, n. 4 (Baehrens, p. 6).

37. Pseudo-Bede, *In psalm.* 8 (PL 93, 527c). Stephen Langton, in Beryl Smalley, *The Study of the Bible in the Middle Ages,* 2nd ed., 1952, p. 262, note.

38. Origen, *In Cantica* (Baehrens, pp. 234–5). 'This immaculate one is pure only because she daily washes in the blood of Christ': Origen as summarized by Hans Urs von Balthasar, *Esprit et Feu,* p. 34. Augustine, *Retract.,* bk. 1, ch. 7, n. 5 (PL 32, 539). Cf. Bardy, *La théologie de l'Église,* vol. 2 (Ed. du Cerf, Paris), pp. 138–9, 162.

39. So Dr. Skydsgaard, in *Le dialogue est ouvert,* vol. 1 (French edition, 1965). Cf. Jer 13:23; Ex 2:4–9, etc.

there was 'an uninterrupted commerce, dialogue, and communion between a holy and faithful God and an impure, faithless people'; but under the New Covenant 'the holy and faithful God of Israel himself brings on the scene for all time a holy and faithful partner . . . raised from the womb of his people', a representative of both God and man in whom for all time God and man are united, Jesus Christ.[40] And, in the same strain, W. A. Visser't Hooft: 'The coming of Jesus Christ is much more than just a new and important chapter in the recital of God's relationship with his people; it is no less than the crashing through of a new age, of an entirely new era which is the kingdom of God, the era of the new creation'.[41] And yet, in the opposite sense, we must not forget that a Church 'which would be only the body of Christ, that is, an expression of the unifying force, to the neglect of the element of resistance to this force, is unthinkable in this century; more than unthinkable, contradictory'.[42] Indeed, to the extent that we consider only the men who make her up, the history of the Church might be summed up 'under this sign also: namely, as the story of all the compromise replacements she has offered God to escape making the act of real faith'.

(2) Another dialectical pair: the Church is at once visible and invisible, at once the Church of authority and the Church of the Spirit—and necessarily so, to judge from the outline of the mystery which we examined when beginning. Neither of these two complementaries should be sacrificed to the advantage of the other. The mystery, the efficacious sign, is not separated from that which it signifies and, on the other hand, what is signified can only be grasped through meditation on the sign.

40. *Introduction à la théologie évangélique* (French edition, Geneva, 1962), pp. 21-2. All of which does not prevent us from saying (with Barth again): 'This history (of the Church), where belief and unbelief, error and superstition, the confession and denial of Jesus Christ, the deformations and the renewals, are all close neighbours, is that of the obedience and disobedience, covert and overt, of Christians to the gospel' (p. 142). See also Dom Vonier, 'Le Peuple de Dieu' and A. Jaubert, 'L'image de la Vigne' in *Oikonomia* (Hamburg 1967), pp. 93–9.

41. *Le renouveau de l'Église* (Labor et Fides, Geneva, 1956), p. 19.

42. Hans Urs von Balthasar, *La gloire et la croix* (French edition, Aubier, Paris, 1967), vol. I, 1965, p. 441. *Qui est chrétien?* (Salvator, Mulhouse, 1967), p. 76. G. Martel has devoted several chapters of his book *Sainteté de l'Église et vie religieuse* (Prière et Vie, Toulouse, 1964) to this complex idea; see also *Les idées maîtresses de Vatican II, Introduction à l'esprit du Concile* (Desclée de Brouwer, Paris, 1967), pp. 77–91.

Here too we see straightaway, without any great need to labour the point, the sort of ecclesiological theory that founders on this particular rock.[43] The Church in its very visibility 'constitutes the Christian experience'.[44] Nothing in the Old Testament suggests the notion of an invisible Church. We shall not reduce the mystical body of Christ to equivalence with the forms of the Roman Church, nor will we water down the Church until it becomes a 'body' conceived in an entirely 'mystical' fashion. What we shall affirm is that the Church mysteriously transcends the limits of her visibility, that by her very essence she carries herself, as it were, above herself. As Hans Urs von Balthasar has explained it, the Church is not the spouse of Christ, nor will she be recognized as such, except in that overreaching which is her love; in what is most urgent and intimate in it Christian love reaches far beyond what we generally refer to as 'Christianity'—and yet, this very reaching beyond, we must add with von Balthasar, *is* Christianity itself.[45] It is the action of the Spirit of Christ, operating in the bosom of the Church. Karl Rahner has also said this and in much the same terms: 'Unlike ideology which is incapable of surpassing itself, Christianity is in a certain sense more than itself: it is, in fact, that movement of man abandoning himself to the mystery at the ground of his being, a mystery that forever eludes him, but with the certainty that this movement leads on to the mystery realized effectively in Jesus Christ: a love making its presence felt, enveloping his existence'.[46]

(3) Finally, the Church is both of this earth and of heaven, historical and eschatological, of time and of eternity. This, basically, is the reason why no short answer is possible to the question, 'does the Church exist for the world, or the world for the Church?' The ambiguity does not only proceed from the ambiguity of the word 'world'. The character of the Church herself is twofold. Both parts of the question may receive *at the same time* the affirmative 'yes', provided both are placed in their inverse perspective. To cling to the first is to risk dissolving the

43. Cf. Luther: *Abscondita est Ecclesia, latent sancti* (WA 18, 652).

44. Rudolf Schnackenburg, *L'Église dans le Nouveau Testament* (French edition, Ed. du Cerf, Paris, 1965), p. 15.

45. Cf. below, ch. 6.

46. 'Is Christianity an Ideology?' in *Concilium*, 6, 1965.

Church into the world, and the danger of such a 'secularization' is particularly acute today. To stress the second is to adhere to a position as anti-Christian as it is anachronistic.

The Chruch, in her present reality and under her present form, must be through all her members at the service of the world; but for the saving of this world, that is, leading it to its destiny, this is the Church again though in her future reality and definitive shape. And even this manner of speaking is inadequate, in that the impression is given of some separation between the Church of today and the Church of the future. With a little more precision, then, let us say, borrowing the words of Jean Mourroux, that 'the time of the Church is inextricably linked with the time of the world and this defines a permanent dimension of the Christian drama; but the time of the cosmos was made with a view to this final linking which will endure when the figure of this world shall have passed.[47]

And here is posed the related problem of the connection of the Church with the kingdom of God. It is as impossible simply to identify the two (however that might be done), as it is to disassociate them.[48] It has been remarked that on this question St. Augustine seems to oscillate 'between two extremes': in some passages, it is said, he speaks of the Church as being, in practice, identical with the kingdom of God (as in *The City of God*, bk 20, ch. 9);[49] in other passages (as in the *Treatise on holy Virginity*, ch. 24)[50] he treats such an opinion as an absurd presumption. This problem has been extended to the full area of Christian tradition so that it has seemed possible to declare that

47. Jean Mourroux, *Le Mystère du temps* (Aubier, Paris, 1962), p. 193. Cf. my *Images de l'abbé Monchanin* (Aubier, Paris, 1967), pp. 109–12.

48. 'The ambiguity inherent in the Church is explained by its active relationship to the kingdom' (Erik Peterson's article 'L'Église' in *Dieu vivant*, 25, 1953, p. 109).

49. N. 1: *Ergo et nunc Ecclesia regnum Christi est regnumque caelorum (Oeuvres de saint Augustin*, Desclée de Brouwer, Paris, vol. 37, p. 234).

50. *Quid aliud istis restat, nisi ut ipsum regnum caelorum ad hanc temporalem vitam, in qua nunc sumus, asserant pertinere? Cur enim non in hanc insaniam progrediatur caeca praesumptio? Et quid hac assertione furiosius? Nam etsi regnum caelorum aliquando Ecclesia etiam quae in hoc tempore est, appellatur, ad hoc utique sic appellatur, quia futurae vitae sempiternaeque colligitur (ibid.*, vol. 3, p. 240). ('What else remains for them but to assert that the very kingdom of heaven pertains to this temporal life we now lead? Why should blind presumption stop at even this lunacy? And is there anything more maddening than such an assertion? For if the temporal Church is sometimes called the kingdom of heaven, certainly it is only because the Church is orientated to the future and eternal life'.)

'this uncertainty has never been dissipated in Roman Catholic theology'.[51]

In reality, going to the heart of the matter, neither uncertainty nor contradiction is involved. Moreover, a careful re-reading in their contexts of the two passages from St. Augustine shows them to be in complete accord. It is simply a case of two contrasted aspects, both inherent in the mystery of the Church. Here, too, we meet a dialectical pair whose mutual extremes must be safeguarded.[52]

For all that, it remains impossible to choose between a so-called 'historical' and 'eschatological' concept of the Church. In the last analysis we must declare simultaneously that (a) our Church is a militant one, she lives on this earth in a constant and truceless war waged with the forces of light against ever-recurring evil, and that (b) she is already, here below, that haven of peace, that dwelling place where God is in residence who, in St. Bernard's phrase, *'tranquillus, tranquillat omnia'*. Both, I repeat, are true *simultaneously,* are genuine part and parcel of enduring reality. When, at the close of a long and sorrowful quest, John Henry Newman decided to become a Catholic, he entered, he tells us, into the Church as into the heavenly Jerusalem, 'blessed vision of peace'.[53]

To conclude, let us say again, with Rudolf Schnackenburg: 'The relation of the Church to the glorified Lord, the life she receives from him, her aspiring towards him, are all beyond the embrace of thought: it is the deepest mystery of the Church'.[54]

51. W. A. Visser't Hooft, *Le renouveau de l'Église*, pp. 35–7. The same reasoning might be applied to the two connected notions in Augustine, the Church and the city of God: cf. *Oeuvres de saint Augustin*, vol. 37, 774-7, and note 28, by F.–J. Thonnard.

52. An analogous observation might be made on the two ways in which Augustine and others comment on the relations between the two Testaments: cf. my *L'écriture dans la tradition* (Aubier, Paris, 1966), ch. 3, §3, 'La dialectique chrétienne'.

53. *Essay on the Development of Dogma*. In the 1877 edition of *Via Media*, Newman devoted several pages to the 'internal contradictions' of the Church. As usual, his point of departure is a natural analogy: 'Whatever is great, refuses to be reduced to human rule, and to be made consistent with its many aspects with itself . . . And how full of incongruities, that is, of mysteries, in its higher and finer specimens is the soul of man . . . We need not feel surprise then if Holy Church too, the supernatural creation of God, is an instance of the same law' (*Via Media*, vol. 1, p. xciv).

54. *L'Église dans le Nouveau Testament*, p. 196. Cf. C. Philips, 'L'Église sacrement et mystère' in *Ephemerides theologicae lovanienses*, 42, 1966, pp. 405-14.

3

Lumen Gentium
and the Fathers of the Church

I

Compare the Constitution *Lumen Gentium*—and, indeed, for that matter the Constitution *Dei Verbum*—with the schema drawn up by the preparatory commission and the contrast is quite astonishing. The result of this has been an impression of novelty expressed, perhaps, with an occasional exaggeration. What was forgotten was that the theology of the preparatory schemata did not fully reflect the state of contemporary theological thinking. In reality, the two doctrinal constitutions of Vatican II merely give the Church's blessing to an effort of reflection over a long period which had appeared in numerous publications from diverse sources and schools of thought, and aimed at many different types of reader.

However, the impression of novelty is not entirely unjustified. No more in the doctrinal elements than in its practical orientations (I speak here of such as may truly claim to be conciliar) was Vatican II a 'conservative' council. But here it is important to distinguish between two epithets which tend to be confused: conservative does not mean traditional; it *could* mean the exact opposite. On some important issues, the ecclesiology of *Lumen Gentium,* far from conserving them, overthrows certain positions formerly held by a school which could, on occasion, almost declare itself the representative voice of official teaching. Its reasons for doing this, however, were to uncover or reestablish more firmly views with more authentic basis in tradition. In this case as in others 'the reform envisaged by the Council does not, therefore, represent a complete upheaval in the present life of the Church. Nor does it desire a rupture with all that is essential and long-established in tradition. Rather it is a homage paid to this tradition while wishing to rid it of all that is invalid or defective in it, thereby restoring its authenticity and fecundity'.[1] In particular it is clear that the promulgated text is in harmonious accord, both in spirit and letter, with the teachings of the Fathers of the Church.

The quite considerable number of its patristic quotations or references has not gone unremarked. Leaving aside the numerous canonical or liturgical texts of the period, there still remain, respectively, in the eight chapters of the Constitution 17, 30, 51, 3, 16, 3, 4 and 27 citations or references.[2] And while a Melkite bishop[3] could fault the original schema (which was very long) for the fewness—only five—of quotations from the Eastern Fathers, the promulgated text gives nearly forty. Not all, of course, carry the same weight; some were concerned with minor details only and some were purely parenthetical. The pertinence or value of this one or that might be disputed. But then the editors of the different chapters, however exhaustive the care they brought to their task, had no wish to line the bottom of each page with a battery of footnotes. And even if they had so wished, their normal conditions of work in the Eternal City during the four years of the Council would not have permitted it.[4] At all events it is not on this purely material and quantitative aspect that we wish to dwell.

Another thing we ought not forget is the relative newness of systematic ecclesiology. It has been in preparation, piece by piece—if one may so phrase it—since the dawn of modern times in the West. If it was true, as had frequently been said in the course of the last fifty years, that the twentieth century would go down in history as 'the century of the Church', it was no less true that those who said so were then still watching the

1. Paul VI, opening address at the second session of the Council (1963). Quite often, observes A. Wenger, 'the bishops who had been classed progressives were more judicious (than the others) in their use of arguments drawn from Scripture and tradition' (*Vatican II, Chronique de la deuxième session,* p. 37, note 3).

2. Counting all the texts from the patristic age, M. Pellegrino arrives at a total of 184 quotations or references ('L'étude des pères de l'Église dans la perspective conciliaire' in *Irenikon,* 1965, p. 454).

3. Mgr. G. Hakim, Archbishop of St. John of Acre, 6 December 1962.

4. Apropos Schema 13, Pellegrino, *loc. cit.,* p. 458 (note), observes that the *Epistle to Diognetus* is cited there 'in the Migne edition, alas! As though Funk, Meecham and Marrou had never existed'. No doubt the explanation is that at the time the editor only had the Migne edition at hand. If so, it was regrettable.

effort of explanation and systematization; this striving for objectivity and completeness was accentuated by the pressure of circumstances joined to a certain drive of inner logic and has only just climaxed in the Constitution which we now have.[5]

Without claiming to be a complete treatise, *Lumen Gentium* shows a certain similarity, in its structure, to a treatise. Obviously, it goes without saying that nothing of its like will be found in the literature of the patristic age. 'The (ancient) councils saw no need to give dogmatic expression to the idea which the Church had of her own nature',[6] any more than did the ecclesiastical writers. Surprise at the absence, in a work such as the *Peri Archon,* of a chapter specially devoted to the Church would show a peculiar lack of the historical sense in the historian of Christian doctrine. It would be expecting too much, therefore, to hope for a perfect parallel between *Lumen Gentium* of Vatican II and the outlines contained in the writings of the Fathers.[7]

Is this to say that the Fathers would not have had concise ideas on this reality, the Church? Or that all they have to offer on the subject are marginal indications—vague, scattered and purely occasional? Far from it. If, after many centuries, the Church is today attempting to look herself in the eye, with a view to undertaking her own definition, the movement is rather one of tying the knot on bootlaces that were already there. Certain people have persuaded themselves that the modern Church has been cutting herself off from the first objects of her faith (which, in the beginning had occupied her thoughts entirely) only to indulge in narcissism. Taking their cue from Auguste Comte and other philosophers, they have wished to see in this a sign of the passage from transcendence to immanence, the decisive passage that characterized the evolution of human thought.[8]

Truth to tell, some members of the Church might be said to

5. See my *Méditation sur l'Église* (2nd ed., 1953), ch. 1, pp. 9-21.

6. Christopher Butler OSB, *The Idea of the Church.* Cf. Gustave Bardy, *La théologie de l'Église de saint Irenée au concile de Nicée* (Ed. du Cerf, Paris, 1947), pp. 7-8. Yves Congar OP in *L'Église de Vatican II,* vol. 1, 1966.

7. Paul VI, opening address at the second session: 'Beyond doubt, it is a desire, a need, a duty of the Church to finally define herself fully . . . There is nothing to be surprised about if, after twenty years . . . the authentic, profound and complete notion of the Church . . . still needs a more precise expression'.

8. See my preface to *L'Église de Vatican II* (Ed. du Cerf, Paris, 1966).

have furnished some grounds for such an interpretation. But, in reality, by means of a new method, by means of a 'reflex action' which is, right enough, 'characteristic of modern man's mentality',[9] the Church is returning more explicity to what was formerly *the* great object of her contemplation. The writings of the Fathers do not have special chapters on the Church because, quite simply, for them the Church was everywhere. She was, as they saw it, the condition, the milieu, and the end of Christian life. They saw her intimate connection with all mysteries, or better, with the entire mystery of faith.

Now here precisely is one of the merits, without doubt the principal merit, of this new Constitution: it shows a constant concern to relate the truths about the Church to dogmatic truth as a whole (unlike what a certain current teaching had formerly been doing). Vatican II remembered the advice of Vatican I: in order to penetrate as far as possible into knowledge of the faith, it systematically carried out one of the essential procedures— considering the connections of the mysteries among themselves.

From the age of the Fathers to that of Vatican II there have been many changes of stress and viewpoint. Responding to new situations, certain features, formerly underlined, are now played down somewhat while other aspects are clarified. Thus, for instance, the theme of the *Ecclesia ex Judaeis* and *ex Gentibus* has died a natural death: the Fathers were still commentating very literally on St. Paul for whom 'the mystery of Christ' wore this precise form in those most urgent and pressing times.[10] On the other hand it was no less natural that the question of the juridical status of the hierarchy vis-à-vis both the Christian communities and the secular power should have loomed large. More recently the newly-acquired consciousness of the real dimensions of human history and the situations brought about by the great schisms have given rise to a concern for distinguishing between the possible degrees of belonging to the Church, etc.[11]

Clearly, too, the teaching of the Fathers is not a uniform monolith. Even a brief acquaintance with the details of their individual thinking shows infinite diversification. We therefore have no

9. Paul VI, *Ecclesiam suam*, 6 August 1964, n. 30.

10. Compare Eph. 2:14–18 and 3:1–6. Cf. André Feuillet, *Le Christ Sagesse de Dieu d'après les Épîtres pauliniennes* (Gabalda, Paris, 1966), pp. 292–3, 302–3.

11. See *infra*.

choice here but to sketch in broad outlines and to determine the means by which the main analogies—and differences—may be set in relief. For the rest, fascinating though the analysis of the details would be and however essential for historical studies, in the context of our present task all that must occupy second place.[12]

II

THE CHURCH AS MYSTERY

The Church is first of all a mystery of faith. *Lumen Gentium* (no. 5, *Ecclesiae sanctae mysterium*) and the Fathers are at one on this. She is a gift from above and human reason must acknowledge its limits in her regard. It is, besides, superfluous to insist on such evidence as reason may offer: the *fact* has imposed itself on every believer in every century.

Equally pointless is an insistence on that other fact—though a passing reference is valuable—namely, that this mystery of the Church is not that of some purely spiritual ideal or invisible reality, without a tangible structure, but is a communion that at least in one of the qualities that constitutes her is a visible society, organized and possessing a power of government.[13] The Church is the 'visible and mystical body of Christ'.[14] She is 'instrument, sign, and sacrament of union with God and of the unity of all human kind' (n. 1).[15] There is no sentence in the Constitution that does not state or suppose this, with the desired nuances in the application.[16] Contemporary Catholic ecclesiology can furnish material for many an argument. But we must recognize that, as Bishop Butler has newly re-established, her continuity on this fundamental point is perfect: the ecclesiology of the first Christian centuries says no different.

12. Cf. J. Ratzinger, *El concepto patristico de la Iglesia* in *Naturaleza salvifica de la Iglesia* (DOC, Ed. Estela, Barcelona, 1965). On the Council, collegiality and the Fathers of the Church, see G. Martelet, *Les idées maîtresses de Vatican II*, pp. 30–41.

13. Cf. Butler, *op. cit.,* pp. 91–3. Schnackenburg, *L'Église dans le Nouveau Testament,* pp. 141–4.

14. Paul VI, opening address at the second session of Vatican II.

15. 'Ursakrament' (Cardinal Frings), 'primordial sacrament' (Mgr. Guano, Leghorn).

16. Thus in n. 8: *Haec Ecclesia, in hoc mundo ut societas constituta et ordinata, subsistit in Ecclesia catholica . . .*

All the criticisms directed against the very principle of the 'institution' fall foul of this first truth. Origen, for instance, is not talking about a completely invisible Church when he terms the greatest misery of all 'being cut off from the mystery of the Church'.[17] In her very visibility the Church 'is constitutive of the Christian experience'.[18] Not so long ago a Lutheran writer, Dietrich Bonhoeffer, forcefully recalled as much. Following the 'ancient Church', whose sturdy scriptural exegesis he praises, Bonhoeffer believes that if one is a Christian 'it is not in an invisible Church that one believes, the kingdom of God considered as *coetus electorum*; we believe that God has made of the empirical, concrete Church—in which is exercised the ministry of word and sacrament—his community; we believe that this Church is the body of Christ, that is, the presence of Christ in the world; we believe, as we have been promised, that the Spirit of God acts in her'.[19]

But full justice is done to her mystery. The relation between her origin and the Trinity is explicity recalled in one or two passages of the Constitution in phrases culled from St. Cyprian.[20] References to the Holy Spirit are more numerous—about a dozen or so[21]—but notwithstanding the fine development in n. 4 most of them are fleeting; they give the impression of being added almost as an afterthought. This is scarcely to be wondered at since the theology of the West, inevitably predominating at the Council, has not developed along pneumatological lines: at least in its most classic mainstream it has tended to forget that 'the time of the Church, in salvation history, is called by the Fathers the Economy of the Spirit'.[22]

17. *Sel. Jo.*, 20, 15 (PG 14, 1036a). Cf. *Peri Archon*, 4, 2, 2 (Koetschau, p. 308).

18. Schnackenburg, *op. cit.*, p. 15. Cf. Jean Colson, *Les fonctions écclésiales aux deux premiers siècles* (Desclée de Brouwer, Paris–Bruges, 1966). Pierre Grelot, *Le ministère de la nouvelle alliance* (Ed. du Cerf, Paris, 1967).

19. *Sanctorum communio* (new ed., Munich, 1954), p. 210. Cf. *Gesammelte Schriften*, vol. 4 (Munich, 1961), p. 256, in René Marlé, *Dietrich Bonhoefer, témoin de Jésus-Christ parmi ses frères* (Castermann, 1967), pp. 48, 49 and 60.

20. Tertullian could also have been quoted: *De baptismo*, c. 6; *De pudicitate*, c. 21.

21. In n. 4, 9, 11, 12, 13, 15, 17, 48 and 50.

22. Mgr. Ignace Ziadé, Maronite Archbishop of Beirut, at the second session of the Council. And at the third session, 16 September 1964, he said: 'The Latin Church's christology is very advanced, but its theology of the Holy Spirit is still at the stage of adolescence'. On the same day Bishop Butler was again regretting the silence on the Holy Spirit, mentioned, he said, only twice, 'and then in a calamitous fashion'.

In compensation, the Eucharist is fully, if sporadically, exploited (a happy legacy from the Fathers this) not only as the source and summit of the Christian life (n. 13) but as the inner force in the Church's make-up (n. 3, 11, 26, etc.).[23] If, according to a favourite phrase of the Orthodox, the Church of Christ is a 'eucharistic communion' then here is solid ground for rapprochement between East and West. The Constitution owes its strength to a central doctrine of our faith, a doctrine which the Latin tradition received from the Fathers[24] and which for long was held in high honour. Thomas Aquinas summed it up when he said that the mystical body which is the Church is the *res* of the sacrament of the Eucharist.[25] Though often recalled since then by theologians of each generation—by Cardinal Franzelin, for example, in his Roman lectures of the last century—its relief in recent centuries has been, generally speaking, blurred.

Only this eucharistic growth did not entail, in the view of the Fathers, a real priority of the local church over the universal. It is quite true that for them 'the local eucharistic community is a manifestation of the whole Church'[26] and that 'each of these communities is the real actualization of the entire universal Church'.[27] But it is no less true that they considered the churches scattered throughout the world as making up the whole body, the sole body 'of the synagogues of the Church', as Origen puts it.[28] It is no accident that the Greek (and Hebrew) word for 'church' applies to both the one and the other.[29] No more than the local church is a mere department of the universal Church, is

23. See again n. 7, 13, 28, 34, 50. The Fourth Lateran Council, in its Decree of 30 November 1215, n. 1, on the Catholic faith, said: 'There is but one Church . . . in which Christ himself is at once priest and victim'. This mention hardly justifies Mlle Raymonde Foreville's speaking of the 'eucharistic character of the Church' and the 'ecclesiology of communion': *Latran I, II, III et IV* (Ed. de l'Orante, Paris, 1965), p. 282.

24. Cf. St. Augustine, *Contra Faustum*, bk. 12, ch. 20 (PL 42, 265); *De Civitate Dei*, bk. 22, ch. 17 (PL 41, 779); *Sermo* 57, n. 7 (PL 38, 389), etc.

25. *Summa Theol.*, III, q. 73, art. 3: *Res sacramenti (eucharisticae) est unitas corporis mystici, sine qua non potest esse salus: nulli enim patet aditus salutis extra Ecclesiam.*

26. Olivier Clément, *L'Église orthodoxe* (1965), p. 7.

27. Mgr. E. Schick, Auxiliary Bishop of Fulda, during the second session (1963), on the importance of the local church.

28. *In Matt.*, 13,24.

29. Cf. Lucien Cerfaux, *La théologie de l'Église suivant saint Paul* (Ed. du Cerf, Paris, 1942). The community of Jerusalem is 'the Church of God', virtually unique; St. Paul also speaks of 'the churches'.

the latter simply a federation composed of the local churches. For there is but one Eucharist, as there is but one baptism and one episcopate. 'As Christ has instituted it', says St. Cyprian, 'there is only one Church spread in several members through the entire world',[30] and in so saying he did not found a new ecclesiology.

The early Church, Latin and Greek, never lost sight of this one Church.[31] Now in this, too, our Constitution is faithful to the patristic tradition.[32] If, in chapter 3, n. 23, the local church is called *'portio Ecclesiae universalis'*, such an expression (though disputable in itself, it may be justified in certain regards) does not pretend to be a full definition; nor is it said that the sacramental communities are *only* parts of the Church. Moreover, in the same n. 23, the explanation is given that the individual churches 'are formed in the image of the universal Church' and that 'it is in and by these that the one and unique Catholic Church exists'.

Any lingering doubts are dispelled when in n. 26 the Constitution declares that 'the Church of Christ is truly present in all legitimate local groups of the faithful who, united with their pastors, also receive, in the New Testament, the name of churches'; and that 'in these communities, so poor and fragile that they may often be dispersed, Christ is present, by virtue of which the Church is constituted one, holy, catholic, and apostolic'. To oppose the ideas of 'sacrament' to 'mission', or, 'the local church, foundation of primitive ecclesiology' to 'Roman universalism' would be to adopt a one-sidedness equally out of harmony with the Fathers as with *Lumen Gentium*.[33]

30. *Epist.* 55, 24, 2. Origen, *In Genesim*, hom. 12, n. 3. (Baehrens, p. 108), etc. On this primacy of the universal Church, see Butler, *The Idea of the Church*. Cf. Gal. 3:27–28; 1 Cor. 10:17, etc.

31. Cf. G. Brady, *En lisant les Pères* (1933), p. 103.

32. Whence follows the great problem of ecumenism which is, as Paul VI told the observers in St. Paul outside the Walls, on 4 December 1965, that of 'the reintegration into the unity of the visible Church of all who bear the happiness and responsibility of calling themselves Christians'.

33. Cf. Meyendorff, *Orthodoxie et catholicité* (1965), pp. 97–8 and 146. One will find in *L'Église de Vatican II*, pp. 607–38, a chapter contributed by Dom Burkhard Neunheuser OSB on *Église universelle et Église locale*. On the eucharistic and local ecclesiology of Fr. Afanassieff, and Fr. Meyendorff's attempt at synthesis, see Hilaire Marot, 'Premières réactions orthodoxes aux décrets de Vatican II' in *Concilium*, 14, pp. 132–41.

Receiving less emphasis in *Lumen Gentium* is another kind of universality which involved the Fathers in difficulties with the notion of the visible Church. Only one explicit allusion is made to it (in n. 2), when treating of the end of the world: *Tunc autem, sicut apud sanctos Patres legitur, omnes justi ab Adam, 'ab Abel justo usque ad ultimum electum', in Ecclesia universali apud Patrem congregabuntur.* ('Then, as we read in the holy Fathers, all the just since Adam, "from the just Abel to the last of the elected", will be assembled in the bosom of the Father in the universal Church.') This almost total abandoning of the old idea of 'the Church of the saints'[34] does not really constitute an infidelity; in fact, it results from a concern for the precision and unification of the concept. This concern imposed itself as soon as the idea of the Church, no longer diffuse and scattered, began to be the object of some measure of systematic reflection.

By compensation, however, the stress now falls more heavily on yet another sort of universality, another sort of openness. Not content to affirm, with the uninterrupted tradition of the Church, that all men 'are called to the catholic unity of the people of God', *Lumen Gentium* goes on to add that, as of now *'ad eam variis modis pertinent vel ordinantur sive fideles catholici, sive alii credentes in Christo, sive denique omnes universaliter homines, gratia Dei in salutem vocati'* (n. 13) ('to this unity belong—or are ordained—in different ways all the Catholic faithful, all those who believe in Christ and, finally, all men without exception whom the grace of God calls to salvation').

Measured phrases these but pregnant with consequences; they do actually lead to a long development (n. 14–17). This section comprises, as is well known, one of the major departures from the preparatory schema. Paul VI had prepared the way for it when, in his speech at the opening of the second session (29 September 1963), he spoke of 'the separated (*disjuncti*) brethren who are also called to full membership of the Church (*ad plene adhaerendum*)'.[35] It represents the fruit of a long reflection, only germinal at the time of the Fathers—necessarily so, since whether touching on the salvation of non-Christians or, even more, on

---

34. The theme reappears, in somewhat different forms, in other conciliar texts.

35. On this, three interventions were decisive: that of Cardinals Lienart and Frings in December 1962, and that of Cardinal Lercaro on 3 October 1963, during the discussion on the first chapter.

the spiritual ties uniting all the baptized believers in Jesus Christ, they arose from a situation of fact created by the schisms of history.[36]

Finally, is there any need to remark that the welding of the mystery of the Church to that of Christ is in perfect continuity with patristic thought? The matter had been raised by Cardinal Montini in his intervention of 4 December 1962: he complained that the preparatory schema 'has not sufficiently brought out the close rapport of the Church with its head, Christ'.[37] In this regard the opening words of the Constitution are eloquent; they determine the key in which all the rest will be written. Contrary to a modern usage which, proceeding by abstractions, seemed occasionally to convey the impression that the Catholic Church posited in herself the source of the Light proposed to men,[38] and conforming to the example set by Paul vi in the opening words of the first encyclical, *Ecclesiam Suam* (i.e. Christ's Church), this beginning places us straightaway in the climate wherein all the rest will be written: *'Lumen gentium cum sit Christus . . .'*[39]

III

THE PEOPLE OF GOD

The preparatory schema stressed the notion of the body of Christ, in continuity with the encyclical *Mystici Corporis* of Pius xii, itself the product of a doctrinal and spiritual movement to which it lent a slightly ambiguous approbation. *Lumen Gentium* stresses much more the notion of the people of God.

36. Cf. K. E. Skydsgaard, 'Le mystère de l'Eglise' in *Le Dialogue est ouvert*, 1 (1965), pp. 155–6. Christopher Butler, 'Rapports entre les crétiens non catholiques et l'Église' in *L'Église de Vatican II*, pp. 653–7. On the study of the Fathers and ecumenism: M. Pellegrino. *loc. cit.,* pp. 460–61.

37. And again Paul vi, inaugurating the second session, called to mind the mosaic in St. Paul outside the Walls in which Honorius iii appears 'tiny, prostrated on the ground, kissing the feet of the immense Christ who is blessing the assembly'. Cf. above, ch. 5.

38. The Church must not 'tarry in any self-complaisance, forgetting Christ from whom she has received everything and mankind to whose service she has been committed . . . She is not an opaque screen . . .': Paul vi, 14 September 1964.

39. Cf. 'Paul vi vu à travers *Ecclesiam suam*' in *Choisir*, Geneva, April 1965.

The determining factor here was the convergence of the views of influential members of the German[40] and French[41] episcopates.[42] It is fair to say that this quite novel orientation must be recognized as one of the major new departures, not only in the Constitution, but in the Council itself. But to what extent does it have patristic warrant?

Certainly ancient texts are not wanting in which the Church is called the people of God.[43] And, following up the logic of such a statement, the Fathers teach the fact of a universal priesthood, common to all the baptized. In this way they declare their opposition to any radical, basic distinction between categories of Christians, repudiating *en bloc* caste theories or any manner of esotericism (one of the features of the pseudognostic heresy). They guard us thus, even today, against the dangers of a unilateral presentation of the relationship between laity and hierarchy, between pastor and flock.[44] It is in this spirit that St. Augustine addresses his audience in one of his sermons: '*Vobis sum episcopus, vobiscum sum christianus*', an expression quoted *infra* in chapter four.

Following the same logic, the whole Church may be said from this point of view to be a sinner;[45] or again, before the distinction between *Ecclesia docens* and *Eclessia docta* intervenes, she will be said, as a totality, to believe, hope, and love; to love her Lord and Saviour and to be awaiting his return.[46] The notion

40. On 6 December 1963, Cardinal Frings, echoing several reputable theologians, had declared: 'Our starting point must be the people of God in pilgrimage; we must avoid a too narrow interpretation of the mystical Body'.

41. Cardinal Garrone was one of the principal editors of this chapter. In the *Dictionnaire théologique* of Louis Bouyer (Desclée de Brouwer, Tournai, 1963) the Church is described first as the people of God (pp. 218–20).

42. Note, however, that a certain fusion of these two important images is achieved in n. 9: *Populus ille messianicus habet pro capite Christum.*

43. They have remained numerous in the liturgy.

44. Some modern documents are not exempt from this fault. Cf. René Laurentin, *Bilan de la troisième session*, pp. 115-6. On the twofold priesthood, cf. my *Méditation sur l'Église* (2nd ed., 1953), pp. 113–22.

45. Cf. Origen, *In Cant. comm.*, 1, 4 (Baehrens, 3, pp. 234–5), etc. Stefan Laszlo, Bishop of Eisenstadt (Austria), made an intervention in the course of the second session, on sin in the Church of God.

46. There are endless texts that might be quoted. Cf. 'La foi de l'Église' in *Christus,* April 1965. Also, in *Dei Verbum*, ch. 2, n. 10, there is no mention of the relationship of Scripture and tradition to the entire Church before the role of the magisterium had been specified.

of the people of God, besides, allows a better understanding of an essential characteristic of the idea of the body of Christ in that it clearly indicates the distance to be kept between the head of the body and the other members. Finally, there can be no doubt at all that viewing the Church as the people of God is implicit at the base of the dynamic, historical 'pilgrim' perspective that was habitual to the Fathers, the Latin Fathers in particular.[47]

All the same, there is a certain argument on this matter that seems to us to carry precious little conviction. During the first four or five centuries, it is sometimes said, the dominant idea of the Church was that of the people of God. Proof is adduced from the origin of the word *Ekklesia,* the Greek translation of the biblical *Qahal Yahweh* or the assembly of the people of God. The observation is correct. *He Ekklesia tou Theou* is indeed 'the People of God'. What does not follow, however, is that when the Fathers used the phrase for the Church they had primarily this orgin and, so, this peculiar signification before their minds. And besides, we must take into account that if 'the idea of the Church has its roots in the Old Testament', her growth was 'in the atmosphere of hellenism' and that 'she is nonetheless neither Jewish nor hellenistic: she is a new Christian creation, she is nothing but Christian'.[48]

On the contrary, when the Church is called the people of God in Christian antiquity the more or less explicit reference is often to the people of the Old Testament. Following St. Paul, the Fathers present the Church of Christ as 'the spiritual Israel' and Christians as the 'true Israelite people', heirs to the prophecies and promises.[49] This is largely the line they take in their treatments of the relation of the Old Testament to the New, though with infinite development and nuance:

The promises made to the patriarchs, the source of the many divine blessings in temporal life, were taken up by the Church

47. The thought of the Latin Fathers was more historical, that of the Greeks more cosmic. Cf. Auguste Luneau, *L'histoire du salut chez les Pères de l'Église* (Beauchesne, Paris, 1964), pp. 8–10. Cf. Philippe Aries, *Le temps de l'histoire* (1954), p. 101: 'Can one help yielding to the temptation to carry this difference of sensibility in regard to ti further than Christianity: to the opposition, vis-à-vis history, of Rome and hellenism

48. N. A. Dahl, quoted by R. Schnackenburg, *op. cit.,* p. 159.

49. Thus St. Justin, *Dialogue with Trypho,* ch. 11, n. 5. See my *Méditation sur l'Église* (2nd ed., 1953); *Catholicisme* (Ed. du Cerf, Paris, 1965), p. 40.

to which was promised not only the present life but life, too, in the centuries to come. Abraham, Isaac, and Jacob no longer belong to the Jews but to the Church. Abraham ,has become the father of all who believe, the story of Isaac signifies that the promise of God no longer depends on birthright but on one's second birth, Jacob is the example of the man chosen by grace . . . Before carnal Israel now rises up the Israel of the Spirit who is in the Church. The carnal Israel, imprisoned in its carnal being, could neither understand nor explain anything but in a carnal manner: the name of the Son, glory, the alliances, the law, cult and the promises. The Church, on the contrary, sees everything from the point of view of its indwelling Spirit: she understands and explains spiritually. The great Spirit-exegesis of the Old Testament by the holy Church, with its symbolism of allegory and type, such as we find already in St. Paul, is not an unimportant and incidental elaboration by the Church to confront Judaism; just as the Church herself is not merely an incidental elaboration to confront the Jewish people. But if the true Israel is the Church and not the Synagogue, then the Church's exegesis of holy Scripture is the true exegesis as opposed to that of the Synagogue.[50]

The Constitution does actually recall this doctrine (in n. 9) but does not delay over it. In this passage from one Testament to the other, from the one people to the other, the Constitution even seems to suggest continuity rather than transformation.[51] The texts therefore do not have quite the same resonance they usually have in the Fathers.

The first Christians certainly used to speak of those who believed in the Bible as 'our fathers, our ancestors'. They held them up as models, as the Epistle to the Hebrews does. The necessity of opposing the 'Gnostics' and the Manichaeans reinforced only all the more their affirmations about the links binding the Church to ancient Israel. Also we are coming to see more clearly the extent to which Jewish prayer influenced the

50. Erik Peterson, *Le mystère des Juifs et des Gentils dans l'Église* (Courrier des Iles, 6; Desclée de Brouwer, Paris, 1936), pp. 4 and 18–19.

51. It is, moreover, especially a question of the editing: cf. n. 9, on the new alliance and the new people.

Christian.[52] But at the same time the Fathers, just as St. Paul and the evangelists before them,[53] saw between the two peoples, as between the two Testaments, an element of opposition alongside the element of prefiguration. Let us conclude, then, in the tradition of the Fathers and the words of J. J. von Allmen: 'theologically speaking, no Israel-Church parallel may be sketched without taking into account that the coming of the Messiah and the infusion of the Holy Spirit placed the people of God in an essentially new position vis-à-vis the old alliance'.[54] Assuredly, this new Israel is not *neos*—but it is *kainos*:[55] the Spirit of Christ has renewed, transfigured, and 'spiritualized' everything.

The Constitution *Dei Verbum* will recall as much, briefly but firmly. If *Lumen Gentium* had underlined it as well, we may be permitted to surmise that its doctrinal equilibrium would have appeared the better for it. Would it be excessive to see in the second chapter the fruit of a happy biblical movement, but one which has not yet fully explored in all its profundity the traditional dialectic between the two Testaments?

In this same matter of the two Testaments, the Fathers and later the medieval theologians piled biblical image on biblical image to suggest many varied aspects of the ecclesial reality. In their very exuberance and diversity they have led to a kind of 'game', its exercise bringing out well their extreme complexity.[56] While the Constitution does mention this—and the mention is

52. Cf. Louis Bouyer, *Eucharistie* (Desclée de Brouwer, Tournai, 1966). Speaking about St. Paul, Bouyer remarks that the Christian soul of prayer is distinguished from the Jewish 'by a mutation whereby expressions of repentance count less than gorgeous language' (p. 26).

53. Cf. J. Coppens, 'L'Église, nouvelle alliance de Dieu avec un peuple' in *Recherches bibliques*, 7, 1965, pp. 13–21. See, for example, Gal. 3:28–29. H. van den Bussche, *L'Église dans le quatrième évangile*. R. Schnackenburg, *L'Église dans le Nouveau Testament*, pp. 70–71, 79–81, 167–76.

54. 'Remarques sur la constitution *Lumen Gentium*' in *Irenikon*, 39, 1966, p. 40, note 1 (criticizing K. E. Skydsgaard). Cf. Pierre Grelot, *Le ministère de la nouvelle Alliance* (Ed. du Cerf, Paris, 1967), pp. 59–63: 'The new Israel, priestly people'. During the Council discussion, Cardinals Siri and Ruffini remarked that the Israelite idea of the people of God was superseded in the New Testament.

55. Cf. Yves Congar, *Chrétiens en dialogue* (Ed. du Cerf, Paris, 1964), pp. 532–3.

56. On the import of these images which are more than just 'illustrations', see Karl Delahaye, *Ecclesia mater chez les Pères des trois premiers siècles* (French edition; Ed. du Cerf, Paris, 1964, pp. 35–53).

valuable as an encouragement to future study[57]—it realized that people of our time expect, especially from an authoritative document, a rather more sober style. A more decisive option was also made. (This was normal, even necessary, given the intention to produce as organic a body of doctrine as possible.) The favoured option was to emphasize the human traits of the Church.[58]

While taken as a whole it is of such a nature as to appeal to Reformed Christians it may conceivably give rise to some uneasiness—though hardly total disagreement—in some Orthodox communions. So it is that the Lutheran writer, Peter Meinhold, believes that 'the declaration of the Church as the People of God, with all the consequences it entails, may facilitate a better understanding among separated Christians';[59] while Mgr. Scrima fears that the interior and divine side of the Church, given from on high and animated by the Spirit, has rather suffered eclipse.[60] Note, however, the significance of the positioning of the chapter on the people of God, a positioning, as is well known, that was not immediately found for it. If it precedes the chapter on the hierarchy—whence the characteristics already remarked on—it has itself been preceded by the chapter on the mystery of the Church and cannot make us forget this. So far

57. Yves de Montcheuil had mentioned this in a lecture he gave on 20 November 1942 to Parisian students on 'L'Église, le Royaume de Dieu et l'Israel nouveau': *Aspects de l'Église* (Ed. du Cerf, Paris, 1949, pp. 18–22).

58. Cf. E. Schillebeeckx OP, *L'Église du Christ et l'homme d'aujourd'hui selon Vatican II* (French edition, 1965), p. 94: 'If we envisage the Church as the people of God . . . she then acquires human traits, the traits of a terrestrial, human event where God has written crooked on a straight history . . . The Church is men who through the saving action of God . . . arrive at a "communion of saints" . . .'; p. 119: more than the idea of the Mystical Body, that of the people of God 'roots the Church more deeply in human history and comes closer to men'.

59. *L'Église de Vatican II* (French ed., 1966), vol. 3, p. 1317. Dr. Skydsgaard also sees in it 'a major advance', and concludes that 'if the developments on the hierarchy are somewhat foreign to the Reformed spirit, as a whole the first four chapters contain many ideas that are *urchristlich*' (*Deutsches Konzilpressezentrum*, 27 November 1963, p. 2). Cf. Yves Congar, *ibid.*, p. 1369: this chapter is 'one of the most promising'.

60. *Ibid.*, p. 1286. However, Archbishop Basil Krivocheine, who has frankly criticized the Constitution more than once, does not appear to be dissatisfied with this chapter: 'Point de vue d'un Orthodoxe' in *Irenikon*, 39, 1966, pp. 477–96. In *L'Église orthodoxe* (1965), p. 65, Olivier Clément presents the Church straight off as the body of Christ, 'an organism whose head is in heaven'. We might remark that *Lumen Gentium* also says (ch. 2, n. 9): 'This messianic people has Christ for its head who . . . now, having taken the name that is above all names, reigns gloriously in heaven'.

as the essentials are concerned, a just equilibrium is thus established.[61]

For the rest, the options of *Lumen Gentium* are not at all exclusive. The image of the temple, for example, and its erection in the Holy Spirit is mentioned in n. 5, but as one among others and is not made the springboard for doctrinal developments. Similarly, though none of the chapters is specifically devoted to the maternity of the Church, the title of mother is several times attributed to her (n. 6, 14, 42, 63). We shall return to this in chapter 7. All the same, we shall remark here that this title was used with more consistency by the Fathers and evoked more precise commentary.

Recall, for instance, the Letter to the Christians of Vienne and Lyons; or the inscription on the Baptistry of St. John Lateran's; or the commentaries on the Vision of the Woman in the Apocalypse; or the many sermons on baptism. Recall, too, Irenaeus speaking of the life-giving faith with which the Church alone, more fecund than the Synagogue of old, nourishes her children;[62] and Hippolytus saying that 'the Church is forever giving birth in her heart to the Logos, Man and God';[63] and Origen wishing that his listeners 'be the joy of their mother, the Church' and fearing that, on the contrary, she must 'still bring forth children in sadness and suffering';[64] and Tertullian celebrating her whom he calls 'Domina mater Ecclesia', '*vera mater viventium*';[65] and Cyprian, laying down the famous principle: 'he cannot have God for father who does not have the Church for mother';[66]

---

61. On the importance of the idea of the people of God for ecclesiology—and its inadequacies when treated alone—one might reread the little book of Dom Vonier, *The People of God*, especially ch. 8. The biblical data are outlined in the article 'Peuple' by Pierre Grelot in *Vocabulaire de théologie biblique* compiled by X. Léon–Dufour, col. 815–26.

62. *Demonstratio*, 5, 94, etc.

63. *De Antichristo*, ch. 61. Also, Methodius on the 'mother forever in labour'.

64. It was his custom to call the Church 'mother'. Cf. Joseph C. Plumpe, *Mater Ecclesia* (1943), pp. 69–80.

65. *Ad martyres*, ch. 1; *De anima*, ch. 10.

66. *De catholicae Ecclesiae unitate*, ch. 6: *Habere jam non potest Deum patrem, qui Ecclesiam non habet matrem*; cf. ch. 5: 'We are her offspring, we are nourished with her milk and animated by her spirit' (*Illius foetu nascimur, illius lacte nutrimur, spiritu ejus animamur*). Ch. 23: 'Whoever cuts himself off from the mother can no longer live or breathe; he loses the substance of salvation'. *Epist.* 74, ch. 7: 'The essential prerequisite for anyone who wishes God for his father is to have the Church for his mother'.

and Cyril of Jerusalem teaching his catechumens that 'Catholic Church is the appropriate name for this mother of us all'.[67] Remember Optatus, Augustine, Fulgentius, Caesarius, all witnessing to their affection for the 'Catholica mater'.[68] The Constitution cites the scriptural texts on which this appellation is based (n. 6) and does them justice in more than one passage. But still its general outlook is otherwise. The idea of the people of God dominates, for the most part, all the succeeding chapters: that on the hierarchy, whose priestly ministry is at the service of the entire people; that on the laity who comprise the greatest number of this people; and even the chapter on religious. When it is speaking of holiness, though the fact that the Church is a sanctifying mother is not forgotten, the exposition of the universal vocation to sanctity receives the fullest treatment. In short, it is a question less of the mother than the children, of the inhabitants rather than the house, of the assembly in Christ (congregatio) rather than the voice that summons (convocatio).

All this is a matter of stress and nuance: no abyss gapes between the two aspects. As Karl Delahaye has well shown in his book investigating the first three centuries and as Fr. Yves Congar explains in the preface,[69] the distinction between the idea of the people of God and that of the Church as mother is not deep. The Ecclesia Mater is not only the hierarchical Church: every holy man engenders the Logos and contributes to its diffusion around him.[70] The perspective the Council chose to adopt may help us see this more clearly.

Nothing of the essentials has been neglected in the abundant but diffuse treasure of patristic writing. A certain choice in leitmotif, however, had to be made. A certain terminology, also corresponding to a certain aspect of reality, was privileged. May we repeat that this was indispensable once the Council had made up its mind to promulgate, if not a definitive treatise, at least an ordered and adjusted body of doctrine. It was also a concern for legitimate adjustment that caused the introduction of some apparently novel developments which, however, add

67. *Catechesis*, 18, ch. 26.
68. The texts will be found in Pierre Batiffol, *Le catholicisme de saint Augustin* (5th ed., 1929), pp. 270–74, etc.
69. *Ecclesia mater chez le Pères des trois premiers siècles*.
70. Cf. my *Exégèse médiévale*, vol. 4 (Aubier, Paris, 1964), the final pages.

nothing radically new to the doctrine. The chief of these is the chapter on the laity, drafted 'on account of special circumstances of our age' (n. 30), and it is much more 'an expressive and realistic tableau of the life of the layman called to make the witness and spirit of Christ shine even in the secular domain'[71] than an exposé of new doctrine. If therefore the two solitary patristic quotations in this chapter—one from St. Augustine, one from the *Epistle to Diognetus*—actually refer to all Christians rather than to the laity as such, there ought to be no reason for surprise.

IV

THE ESCHATOLOGICAL PERSPECTIVE

A perspective that may really be called novel in the light of the classic teaching (though not always of the theological reflections) of these last centuries is the eschatological perspective.

The seventh chapter of the Constitution deals with 'the eschatological nature (*indoles*) of the pilgrim Church'.[72] But, in fact, it is not just the seventh chapter that is so treated but the entire Constitution, from a point of view that is at once collective and dynamic. The Church is the people of God journeying towards a common destiny. Her mission, arising from the universal salvific design, is to realize this in bringing all men together in Christ. Nothing untraditional about that, of course—but, as a whole, the tradition has not been grasped without some difficulty;[73] nor could it easily have been without taking into account a new datum.

To the extent that the Church is an enduring body, her thoughts have also been for those of her members already departed. In her mind, they constituted the 'Church triumphant'

71. Mgr. Gerard Philips, 'La Constitution *Lumen Gentium*' in *Ephemerides theologicae lovanienses,* 1966, p. 32. The instigator was Bishop John Wright of Pittsburgh. 'Many bishops had complained about the absence of a theology of the laity in the schema, but they themselves had not contributed much to a lucid outline of the doctrine': A. Wenger, *Vatican II, chronique de la deuxième session,* pp. 102–3. In fact, all its essential elements might have found a place in a chapter on the people of God.

72. Its editing was delayed and hasty; the project was discussed for only two days, 15 and 16 September 1964.

73. Cardinal Frings had deplored, as early as 30 September 1963, the absence of an eschatological perspective in the new schema.

47

(or the 'Church suffering'), while she herself, on earth, was the 'militant' or 'pilgrim Church'. An important section, consequently, of the seventh chapter treats of the union between the Church here on earth and 'the heavenly Church'. Though one will find traces of this in earliest Christian antiquity, the section remains rather less patristic than the rest; and the title is not at all patristic.

When an Origen wrote, in the fourth book of the *Peri Archon*: 'we must attach ourselves to the rule of the heavenly Church of Jesus Christ according to the apostolic succession',[74] it is clear that for him the 'heavenly Church' is none other than the historical, visible, and even hierarchical Church that lives on this earth. The same may be said of St. Zeno of Verona's introduction of his newly-baptized to 'this heavenly mother who gives you birth, joyful and free'.[75] So, too, St. Irenaeus,had recognized in the present Church, founded by Christ and the apostles, the 'Jerusalem from on high' of which the old, earthly Jerusalem had been the preparation and figure.[76] St. Hilary would say the same, when comparing the mystical body of Christ to a city – by allusion, to the heavenly Jerusalem: 'by our participation in his flesh, we become citizens of this city';[77] and for St. Augustine the Church is this heavenly Jerusalem *'in mysterio'*.[78]

Another manner of speaking, however, supposing another way of looking at things, has prevailed; but the seventh chapter still bears traces of the older: *'Eucharisticum ergo sacrificium celebrantes, cultui Ecclesiae caelestis . . . jungimur'* (n. 50).

Here too, though, we must guard against exaggeration. The relatively new consideration of the links existing or those being forged from moment to moment, if it may so be put, between the two Churches, or two parts of the Church, one on earth, the

74. Bk. 4, ch. 2 (Koetschau, p. 308). Origen also speaks (after Hebr. 12:23) of 'the Church of the firstborn' or 'the firstborn of the heavenly Church', understanding by this the members of the Church 'whose names are written in heaven': *In Luc.*, hom. 7, n. 8; all of which is reasonably close to our modern terminology.

75. *Allocutiones paschales*, 1. Cf. Henri Chirat, *La vie spirituelle*, 1 April 1943, p. 327.

76. *Adversus haereses*, bk. 5, ch. 35, n. 2 (Harvey, 2, p. 146).

77. *In Matt.*, bk. 4, ch. 12 (PL 9, 935).

78. *In psalm.* 148, n. 4 (PL 37, 1940). On this expression and the eschatological situation of the new people of God according to the Epistle to the Hebrews, see R. Schnackenburg, *op. cit.*, pp. 99–105; for the Apocalypse (19:7; 21:2), p. 164.

other in heaven—a consideration incidentally, not entirely absent from patristic writings[79]—does not obscure the consideration of the dynamism that propels the Church towards her eternal destiny: *Peregrinando procurrit Ecclesia, crucem et mortem Domini annuntians, donec veniat* ('The Church proceeds on her pilgrimage . . . announcing the cross and death of the Lord until be comes')—*donec per crucem perveniat ad lucem, quae nescit occasum* ('until, by the cross, she arrives at the light that does not wane') (n. 8 and 9.)

It is in much the same fashion that St. Cyprian expresses himself when he proclaims his hope in the final victory of the Church, to be achieved in the next world.[80] So too St. Gregory the Great, comparing the Church to a city: *'Ipsa civitas, scilicet sancta Ecclesia, quae regnatura in caelo, adhuc laborat in terra'*, etc. All Gregory was doing was repeating in summary form the arguments set forth by St. Augustine at the beginning of his great work *The City of God* (though at this stage the word 'Church' does not figure).[81] Speaking in this way, Cyprian, Gregory, and the others are describing the Church visible, the Church of this life, struggling or on pilgrimage—and in this the Constitution is at one with them.

In other words, considering eschatology from the individual point of view, which had little by little introduced the present duality of the Church on earth and the Church in heaven united 'in the communion of the entire mystical body' (n. 50)—a duality retained in chapter 7 of *Lumen Gentium*—did not suppress the consideration of collective eschatology, showing the people of God being guided, generation after generation, towards, and already mystically united to, the heavenly Jerusalem. More

---

79. The Memento of the Dead, whose language is archaic and to which the *Nobis quoque peccatoribus* was added, is probably very old (Bouyer, *Eucharistie*, pp. 236–8). See also St. Augustine, *Enchiridion*, ch. 15, n. 56: *Ecclesia . . . quae tota hic accipienda est, non solum ex parte quae peregrinatur in terris . . . verum etiam ex illa quae in caelis semper ex quo condita est cohaesit Deo . . . Haec in sanctis angelis beata persistit et suae parti peregrinanti sicut oportet opitulatur.* But the difference is fairly clear to see. *Ibid.*, ch. 29, n. 110; prayer for the dead.

80. Cf. Butler, *op. cit.*, p. 12.

81. Gregory, *In Ezech.*, bk. 2, hom. 1, n. 5 (PL 76, 338d). Augustine, *De Civitate Dei*, prefatio, init.: *Gloriosissimam civitatem Dei, sive in hoc temporum cursu, cum inter impios peregrinatur ex fide vivens, sive in illa stabilitate sedis aeternae, quam nunc expectat per patientiam*, etc.

precisely, this collective journey is described as a march towards unity: the people of God already assembled since the first preaching of the gospel have been assigned its mission—bring all mankind together. On this the most significant text is found, not in the seventh chapter, but in the ninth (n. 9): *Populus ille messianicus, quamvis universos homines actu non comprehendat, et non semel ut pusillus grex appareat, pro toto tamen genere humano firmissimum germen unitatis, spei et salutis* ('This messianic people, though not yet embracing all men and often having the appearance of a small flock, constitutes nonetheless the most potent force for the unity, hope, and salvation of all human kind').

As mentioned earlier, n. 1 had said as much in the first presentation of the Church as 'the sign and instrument of intimate union with God and the unity of all mankind'. And these affirmations receive completeness in the direct evocation of the last end (in n. 36 of the fourth chapter): *Christus, . . . cui omnia subiciuntur, donec Ipse se cunctaque creata Patri subiciat, ut sit Deus omnia in omnibus*[82] ('Christ, . . . to whom all is subject, waits for the day when he himself, with all creation, will be subject to his Father, so that God may be all in all').

The historical march of men to final unity in Christ, the consummation of the universe in God—this twofold trait faithfully reproduces the eschatological thought of the Fathers. The former received perhaps more stress from the Latin Fathers, being more aware, as we have said, of the march of history;[83] the latter from the Greek Fathers, with their more cosmic ethos.[84]

Following the example of Christ, the final unification and consummation presupposes a passage through death and radical transfiguration. This is dealt with at the close of the fifth chapter in the summons of all to sanctity, quoting the warning of the Apostle: *Qui utuntur hoc mundo, in eo ne sistant: paeterit enim figura hujus mundi.* This is repeated in the sixth chapter, devoted to the religious life which 'announces the final resurrection and glory

82. Paolo Molinari sj has collected the principal texts of eschatological flavour in the different chapters: *L'Église de Vatican II*, pp. 1209–15.

83. Neither for the Fathers any more than for *Lumen Gentium*, of course, is it a question of purely temporal history.

84. M. W. Visser't Hooft remarks on this subject that 'it is by the idea of the cosmic import of Christ's victory that Orthodoxy will enrich Western theology': *La royauté de Jésus–Christ* (Geneva 1948), p. 44.

of the heavenly kingdom' (n. 40) and which is developed in the seventh chapter. Right from the start, it proclaims the heavenly, transcendent character of this universal consummation: *Ecclesia . . . nonnisi in gloria caelesti consummabitur, quando adveniet tempus restitutionis omnium, atque cum genere humano universus quoque mundus, qui intime cum homine conjungitur et per eum ad finem suum accedit, perfecte in Christo instaurabitur* (n. 48) ('The Church . . . will only have her consummation in heavenly glory, when the time shall come for the renewal of all things, and when, with mankind, the entire universe itself, intimately united with man and attaining its destiny through him, will find its definitive perfection in Christ.)'

We may well rejoice that in *Lumen Gentium* the traditional and patristic thinking has been thus officially revived. It is the consecration of a theological movement of our century, a movement stimulated and, to some degree, necessitated by the general philosophical climate;[85] but a movement also that was itself a revival of what had been at the heart of Catholic tradition from the beginning and which the liturgy had so faithfully preserved.[86]

But nevertheless it remains true that the Constitution's option of the notion of the people of God as the basic concept, together with present juxtaposition of the two Churches—the terrestrial which we comprise and the heavenly composed of the elect already 'home'—has necessarily led to a certain narrowing of the patristic horizons. 'You stand before Mount Sion, the city of the living God, the heavenly Jerusalem', the Epistle to the Hebrews had said. The Fathers meditated the words in faith. The Church which gave them life in the waters of baptism, this Church—visible and terrestrial herself—was therefore for them

---

85. Here is where the influence of Teilhard de Chardin makes itself felt.

86. On this, let us point out a subtle transposition of thought in the use of an old literary form. The final sentence of the second chapter is worded thus: *Ita autem simul orat et laborat Ecclesia, ut in populum Dei, Corpus Domini et Templum Spiritus sancti, totius mundi transeat plenitudo* . . . ('So does the Church work and pray that the entire world may become the people of God, the body of the Lord, and the temple of the Holy Spirit'). It reproduces, with the modifications necessitated by the context, a liturgical prayer from the Gelasian sacramentary (*Liber Sacramentorum Romanae Ecclesiae*): . . . *Praesta ut in Abrahae filios et in Israeliticam dignitatem totius mundi transeat plenitudo* (ed. H. A. Wilson, Oxford, 1894, pp. 82–3). ('Grant that the entire world may become sons of Abraham and the glory of Israel'). The prayer is still used in the Roman liturgy for the paschal vigil.

at the same time 'the heavenly Church', 'the heavenly Jerusalem, our mother'. 'Live from now on in the Church', St. Augustine says, 'that you may not be rejected in eternity';[87] and again, 'the present-day Church is the kingdom of Christ and the heavenly kingdom'.[88] In this all-embracing view of the mystery the Church is identified with Christ, her spouse, who is himself the kingdom: *'autobasileia'*, as Origen admirably puts it. Now this view corresponds to the deepest logic of Christian eschatology and to depart from it could lead to many abuses of both thought and action. The reign of God is yet to come; but 'without waiting for history to run its course, it has already, in a mysterious antici-pation, made its appearance in the inner marrow of history'. Since the fact of Christ and his resurrection, '"time-after" is already present in the interior of time'.[89]

This is the most mysterious aspect of the Church, the aspect which 'identifies her with Christ and that, in turn, identifies Christ with the kingdom. There is no question of imagining a vague middle terrain between the 'not-yet' and the 'already-present'. Nor is it a question of a half-crossed threshold. In one way, for the people of God envisaged as still on pilgrimage through the obscurity of this world, it is altogether a matter of the 'not-yet'. But in another way—and one that cannot be dis-associated from the first—for the Church considered as a gift from above and the habitation of Christ and his Spirit, we are faced with the 'already-present'.[90]

Choosing the first of these perspectives (though not without complementary indications) did not allow the indiscriminate reproductions of certain expressions found in the Fathers. Con-fusion would have resulted and the Constitution would have been open to the charge of putting the visible aspect of the Church in place of the kingdom, the hierarchy somehow in place of God. There was yet another consequence: to the ques-tion, 'does the Church exist for the world, or the world for the Church?', there can obviously be only one answer: the Church exists for the world. But let us specify straightaway that the two

87. *In psalm.* 124, n. 4.

88. *Sermo* 105.

89. Cf. Butler, *op. cit.*, p. 213.

90. Cf. St. Augustine, *In Johannem*, tract. 81, n. 4: 'What we desire because we live in Christ is quite other than what we desire because we still live in this world' (PL 35, 1842).

opposed answers are contradictory in appearance only. It is, once again, a question of viewpoint.

The words 'Church' and 'world' are neither of them univocal. Insofar as she is visible and temporal, the Church is destined to pass away. She is a sign and a sacrament, and it is the peculiar quality of signs and sacraments to be re-absorbed in the reality they signify.[91] She is a means—divine and necessary—but like all means, provisional. So it was that Pius XI was one day moved to remark: 'Men are not created for the Church, but the Church for men'[92]—*propter nos homines et propter nostram salutem.*

This point of view demands on the part of all the members of the Church, and more especially the hierarchy, an attitude of humble service following the example set them by the Word incarnate who 'did not come to be served, but to serve'. *Lumen Gentium* insists most happily on this, in n. 5 and 8, echoing yet again words of Paul VI, 'the Church is not her own proper end',[93] and, in a way, preparing us for the pastoral teaching of *Gaudium et Spes*. Patristic antecedents are not lacking by which it could have bolstered its case. It was Origen, for instance, who said: 'He who is called to the episcopacy is not called to domination, but to service of the whole Church',[94] and again, this time taking in all men: 'The bishop should be the servant of all by his humility that he may render service to all in the matters that concern salvation. Such is the command given us by the Word of God'.[95]

But, on the other hand, and without the slightest prejudice to that humble service to which he himself gave constant and heroic witness, the Abbé Monchanin could deplore, in the interests of a fuller and deeper understanding of the mystery and in perfect agreement with another aspect of patristic teaching, the 'ravages' of a philosophy that in the end 'defines the Church by reference to the world and no longer the world by reference

91. Cf. *Méditation sur l'Église*, pp. 56–63.

92. Discourse to the Lenten preachers in Rome, 28 February 1927.

93. Opening speech at the third session. Mgr. Huygue (Arras) criticized the first schema as follows: 'The Church is presented as a power . . . Such a spirit . . . was not Christ's. In the Church founded by Christ, does authority mean anything else but the service of others?'

94. *In Cant. comm.*, 1, 3 (Baehrens, 3, p. 117).

95. *Qui vocatur ad episcopatum, non ad principatum vocatur, sed ad servitutem totius Ecclesiae; In Matt. comm.*, bk. 16, ch. 8 (Klostermann–B., p. 493).

to the Church'.[96] In the last century, Dom Gréa had found himself heir of the same teaching, with the same comprehensive vision, when he wrote on the first page of his treatise *De l'Église et de sa divine constitution*:[97] 'The Catholic Church is the beginning of and the reason for all things'.

In the second century Hermas had said the same in the second Vision of his *Pastor*: she resembles, he said, an aged woman 'because she has been the first created, before anything else: it was for *her* the world was made'.[98] Yes, made for the Church, to be assumed into, saved, and transfigured by her. For Origen the Church was the 'cosmos of the cosmos'. For St. Ambrose all the *orbis terrarum* was somehow contained in her womb.[99] Clement of Alexandria would say: 'In the same way that the will of God is an act which we call the world, so his intention is the salvation of man—and this intention we call the Church'.[100] If, from this standpoint, the Church is still other than the kingdom, she must aim to be gathered up into it, as the *Didache* puts it: 'Have a mind, Lord, for your Church. Keep her from all harm. Make her perfect in your love. From the four winds of heaven, gather her whom you have sanctified into the kingdom you have prepared for her'.[101] *Mundus reconciliatus, Ecclesia*.[102]

V

THE CHURCH AND THE VIRGIN MARY

When dealing with the people of God and, more so, when discussing eschatology, we have alluded to this term 'mother' which the Constitution applies to the Church but which it did

96. *Ermites du Saccidânanda* (Casterman, 1956), p. 22.

97. Casterman, Tournai, 1965.

98. *Second Vision*, n. 4, third tableau. Cf. 2 *Clem.*, ch. 14, n. 1, on the 'spiritual Church' which 'was created before the sun and the moon'.

99. *Ingo*, bk. 6, ch. 38 (PG 14, 301). St. Ambrose, *In psalm.* 118, *sermo* 12, n. 25.

100. *Pedagogus*, bk. 1, ch. 6, 27.

101. *Didache*, 10, 5.

102. St. Augustine, *Sermo* 16, n. 8 (PL 38, 588).

not make the principle of a systematic treatment. We shall now find it again, in the last chapter, given over to 'the Virgin Mary in the mystery of Christ and the Church'.

There was much argument, even in the Council itself, before the view prevailed that the schema on the Virgin Mary should be included in the Constitution on the Church. Contrary to what has often been claimed, let us make quite clear that the original intention of the preparatory doctrinal commission had been to do precisely that.[103] The plan to separate the two was adopted by the commission only later when it was clear that the chapter in question had become noticeably longer than the others; that it constituted, in fact, a small *summa* of independent Mariology (something that is not entirely true of it in its definitive version). In any case, the decision of the Council (it had been suggested by the Pope)[104] to view the role of our Lady in the context of the Church had two happy outcomes: it provided a splendid rounding-off for the Constitution and few better means could have been chosen to ensure for chapter seven also a continuity with patristic thought, without detriment to subsequent progress. Also, and most importantly, it allowed the Church to be seen as 'spouse' and 'virginal mother', the patristic theme *par excellence*.

The Church–Spouse, if we are not mistaken, is the object of four passing references in *Lumen Gentium* (n. 6, 7, 9 and 39). The theme is subordinated to that of the people of God, as formerly it had been to that of the mystical body. A pity, because it is every bit as well-founded in Scripture and the Fathers as the other two. 'The Fathers see a mysterious parallel between the creation of the first woman and the birth of the Church.'[105] The analogy of the body, as is only to be expected, often leads them

103. The subcommission *de Ecclesia* met for the first time on 26 November 1960 and decided to prepare a provisional text that would include a chapter on the Virgin: U. Betti OFM in *L'Église de Vatican II*, 1965, vol. 2, p. 59. Historical details in R. Laurentin, *La Vierge au concile* (Ed. du Seuil, Paris, 1965), ch. 1.

104. Opening speech at the second session. Its insertion was specially asked for by Cardinal Frings (Cologne), Silva Henriquez (Santiago de Chile) and Garrone. Cardinal König (Vienna) spoke in its favour and it was carried by a slight majority (1,114 for; 1,074 against) on 29 October 1963.

105. Dom O. Casel, *Le mystère de l'Eglise, union de Dieu et des hommes* (French ed., 1965), p. 55. S. Tromp SJ, *Ecclesia Sponsa, Virgo Mater* (Rome 1937).

(as it had St. Paul)[106] to that of the spouse. 'Christ and the Church are no longer two beings, but one flesh, for it has been said to the spouse: you are the members of Christ' (Origen).[107] 'The Church is the body of Christ, and the mystery of Adam and Eve is a prophecy with direct bearing on Christ and the Church' (St. Hilary).

There are many such texts and they are found in every age of the patristic era and in every milieu, from the 'Second Epistle of Clement the Roman'—which is, in reality, a very old sermon—to St. Augustine and his disciples.[108] All the espousals mentioned in the Bible are interpreted in this sense.[109] We know that since its earliest commentators, Hippolytus and Origen, the Canticle of Canticles has been understood as the wedding-song of Christ and his Church. The second last chapter of the Apocalypse guided the thought of the Fathers.

Now this spouse is mother and she is virgin. The seventh chapter deals with this (in n. 63 and 64) when developing the analogy of the Church and Mary. The Church, which by her preaching and baptism brings forth sons conceived of the Holy Spirit to a new and immortal life, keeps for her virgin, spotless spouse, the faith she has vowed him. A note here sends us back to Ambrose and Augustine. The references could have been multiplied.

The theme of the parallelism between Mary and the Church, wrote Mgr. Gerard Philips in 1963, 'arose in contemporary theology in a manner as unexpected as it is dazzling'. It has not proved, however, to be an arbitrary and passing fashion. 'Far from remaining on the periphery of Christian dogma' with it

106. Cf. Dom Paul Andriessen, 'La nouvelle Ève, corps du nouvel Adam' in *Recherches bibliques*, 9, 1965, pp. 87–109. See also André Feuillet, *Le Christ Sagesse de Dieu d'après les Epîtres pauliniennes*, p. 368.

107. *In Matt. comm.*, bk. 14 (Klostermann–B., p. 326). Cf. *In Cant. comm.*, I, 1, n. 7, etc.

108. See M. Agterberg, '*L'Ecclesia virgo* et la *Virginitas mentis* des fidèles dans la pensée de saint Augustin' in *Augustiniana*, 9, 1959, p. 221–76.

109. An author at the beginning of this century wrote, echoing the misunderstanding of the Fathers' thought, then almost general: 'It is agreed that to dissipate the perfume of scandal from the facts of the Old Testament relative to the prophets, Christian exegesis used to turn their marriages into mysteries': Gabriel Oger, *Les Pères apostoliques*, I, *Doctrine des Apôtres*, 1907, p. 99. Cf. F. Grappin, 'Recherches sur le thème de l'Église-Épouse dans les liturgies et la littérature de langue mystique' in *L'Orient chrétien*, 1958, pp. 317ff. A. Raes, *Le mariage dans les Églises d'Orient* (Chevetogne 1959), Introduction, pp. 13ff.

we touch on 'one of the most important characteristics of Catholic thought'.[110] And it also is, of course, a patristic theme.[111] One understands why the Council wished to retain it. However, as Mgr. Philips again has us remark: 'Mary in the Church is not the prototype of the hierarchical power, but the model of spiritual receptivity to the influx' of divine grace.[112] This may—and should—be understood in two ways or, rather, involves two different consequences. Both are explicitly treated in this final chapter and both are solidly founded in patristic thought.[113]

To begin with, the virgin-motherhood of Mary, the fruit of this spiritual receptivity, is the prototype of the Church's virgin-motherhood with regard to Christians. *In mysterio enim Ecclesiae, quae et ipsa jure mater vocatur et virgo, beata Virgo Maria praecessit, eminenter et singulariter tum virginis tum matris exemplar praebens* ('In the mystery of the Church which also justly receives the title of mother and virgin the blessed Virgin Mary occupies the first place, offering, to an eminent and singular degree, the model of the virgin and the mother'—n. 63 and developed in n. 64 and 65).

St. Ambrose was the first to say this explicitly. Before him Justin and Irenaeus had shown in the Virgin of the annunciation the new Eve; Tertullian and Methodius had shown the Church, true mother of the living, come from the wound in the side of the crucified Christ, as the first Eve come from the side of the sleeping Adam.[114] Ambrose brought both themes together and called Mary the *'typus Ecclesiae'*[115] and was followed in this by

110. In Hubert de Manoir's *Maria*, vol. 7 (Beauchesne, Paris, 1964), pp. 365–6.

111. In an article on Mary as mother and type of the Church (*Osservatore Romano*, 7 February 1964), Fr. Balić OFM wrote: 'All who appreciate the just liberty which was manifested at the Council are certain that theologians will be allowed full freedom to pursue the traditional Christ-typology and the more recent Church-typology in their marian studies'. We agree, but question the exactitude of the opposition between 'traditional' and 'more recent'.

112. *Loc. cit.*, p. 367.

113. Cf. Aloïs Muller, 'L'unité de l'Église et de la Sainte Vierge chez les Pères des IVᵉ et Vᵉ siècles' in *Marie et l'Église*, I (*Bulletin de la société d'études mariales*, 1951), p. 29.

114. Tertullian, *De anima*, ch. 43 (PL 2. 723); Methodius, *The Banquet*, 3, 8 and 18, 8.

115. *In Lucam*, 2, 7 (PL 15, 1555). Cf. G. Philips, *loc. cit.*, p. 368. On Mary as the second Eve in the Fathers, see the fourth chapter in Newman's *On the Cult of the Virgin in the Catholic Church*.

St. Augustine.[116] The expression is found again in St. Ephrem[117] and St. Cyril of Alexandria will say more strongly still:'Mary, that is, the holy Church'.[118] Under this first aspect of the analogy Mary is therefore the figure of the Church insofar as this latter is a sanctifying mother.[119] But the Church is also the people of God, sanctified or on the way to sanctification, an aspect which *Lumen Gentium*, given its basic perspective, could not neglect. We find it outlined in n. 68: *Interim autem Maria, quemadmodum in caelis corpore et anima jam glorificata, imago et initium est Ecclesiae in futuro saeculo consummandae, ita his in terris, quoadusque advenerit dies Domini, tanquam signum certae spei et solatii peregrinanti populo Dei praelucet* ('Just as in heaven where she is already glorified [body and soul] Mary represents and inaugurates the achievement of the Church in the future age, so even on this earth, awaiting the coming of the Lord's day, she shines already as a sign of certain hope and of consolation before the pilgrim people of God'). Earlier the Constitution on the sacred Liturgy had brought up her role in its fifth chapter, 'on the liturgical year' (n. 103): '. . . *in qua (Maria) praecellentem Redemptionis fructum miratur et exaltat (Ecclesia), ac veluti in purissima imagine, id quod ipsa tota esse cupit et sperat, cum gaudio contemplatur'.*

Under this second aspect, Mary, full of grace, prototype of all perfection, is the eschatological figure of the Church, that is, of the entire people of God. From the Middle Ages, and particularly in Marian commentaries on the Canticle of Canticles, the analogy has often been exploited in this sense. Mary—and she alone—appears, by anticipation, as the perfect Church, the final

---

116. *In Johannem*, tract. 13, n. 12 (PL 35, 1499); *Sermones* 191 and 192 (PL 38, 1010, 1012–13). Cf. the *Relatio* of Cardinal König (1963): 'This marian devotion as it is expressed in the litanies of the Blessed Virgin Mary arose historically from the consideration of the Church as mother. All the attributes of the common litany were given to the Church before they were given to the blessed Virgin'.

117. Cf. Muller, *loc. cit.*, p. 29.

118. *Hom. div.*, 4 (PG 77, 992). Muller, *loc. cit.*, pp. 30–31.

119. Cf. *Méditation sur l' Église* (2nd ed.), pp. 279–93. Paul VI, audience of 27 May 1964: 'Ideal image of the Church, as St. Ambrose and after him St. Augustine have said, . . . we find in Mary all the riches that the Church represents, possesses, and dispenses. In Mary we have beyond all else the virginal mother of Christ; in the Church we have the virginal mother of all Christians . . . The prerogatives of the Virgin are communicated to the Church . . .'

communion of all the faithful. It is in the mystery of the assumption, therefore, that the theme finds its full flowering:[120] and it was natural that Pius xII's proclamation of the dogma should have brought it back into favour.[121] But it is a theme that was not wholly absent from Christian antiquity. St. Ambrose had sketched it more than once,[122] applying the principle on which Origen had based his exegesis of the Canticle of Canticles: the symbolization of the Church and the faithful soul or, if you wish, their 'mysterious interpenetration'.[123] If the Church, in the figure of Mary, conceives of the Holy Spirit and gives birth to Christ in her members through the gift of faith and baptism, so too every Christian who, again in the image of Mary, hears, receives, and keeps the word of God, gives birth to Christ. *Ecclesia in sanctis, Virgo mater.*[124]

But this last chapter of *Lumen Gentium* does not limit itself to the analogy between the Church and Mary. The outline is rounded off by indicating the place of the latter in the former, Mary being 'its pre-eminent and altogether unique member' (n. 53). This passage too has not gone unchallenged. The arguments have been somewhat idle and too often partial, in one way or another neglecting precise study of the relevant texts—either the Council's or the Pope's.

On the one hand, the Constitution itself asserts the spiritual maternity of Mary, not only in relation to each of us but (quite unambiguously, it seems to me) in relation to the Church herself: '. . . *eamque (Mariam) catholica Ecclesia a Spiritu sancto edocta, filiali pietatis affectu tanquam matrem amantissimam prosequitur'* ('She is the object on the part of the Church, instructed by the Holy Spirit, of a filial sentiment of piety, as is fitting for a very

---

120. Thus Serlon de Savigny, *In Assumptione*, I. Isaac de l'Etoile, *Sermo* 61 (texts in H. du Manoir, *Marie,* vol. 7, pp. 390 and 438).

121. The Orthodox know it too: thus V. Losski, *Essai sur la théologie mystique de l'Orient* (1944), p. 190.

122. *In Luc.,* 2, 26 (PL 15, 1642; quoted by Paul vI: cf. Laurentin, *La Vierge au concile,* p. 48). And again, *In Luc.,* 7, 5 and 10, 134 (CSEL 32–34, pp. 284 and 506); 2, 7, *In psalm.,* 118, 22, 30 (CSEL 62, 503–04). *Exhort. virg.,* 5, 28 (PL 16, 344). *De institut. virg.,* 14, 87–9 (PL 16, 326).

123. Karl Delahaye, *op. cit.,* p. 192.

124. See the beautiful texts of Rupert de Deutz, quoted by C. Dillenschneider, 'Toute l'Église est dans Marie' in *Marie et l'Église,* 3, 1953, pp. 96–7.

loving mother'—n. 53).[125] A little further on it says again that 'being the mother of Christ and mother of men' Mary occupies in the Church 'the most elevated place after Christ'.[126]

This precisely is what Paul VI had wished for, in his closing speech at the second session, 4 December 1962; in fact it is more, since the Pope had not expressed the wish that the Council itself give this title to Mary.[127] And yet we should note that each time the Pope saw fit to honour our Lady with the title 'mother of the Church' (his desire to do so has been obvious) he hedged it about with a series of qualifying clauses and cautions that tally exactly with the intricate nuances of the conciliar teaching.[128] In particular, his closing speech of the third session, 21 November 1964, 'shows again and again his intention of stating only that which harmonizes with the text of the Constitution'.[129]

There is of course no doubt at all that the expression 'mother of the Church' is firmly grounded in tradition; though to use it in a vacuum and unexplained makes it less so. The first authors to use it associate, as does Paul VI, the two appellations 'mother' and 'daughter'. Thus Berengarius in the eight century, commenting on the Apocalypse: 'Mary is the mother of the Church, because she gave birth to him who is her head; she is a daughter of the Church, because she is a member—the most august member

125. Cf. Paul VI, 11 October 1963, in St. Mary Major's: 'Grant, Mary, that this Church . . . , in defining herself, will recognize you for her mother, her daughter and eminent sister, her incomparable model, her joy and her hope'. 'The spiritual maternity of Mary' furnished the theme of the 8th Marian Congress at Lisieux in 1961.

126. It is, no doubt, to this passage alone that Fr. Wenger refers when he writes: 'The Council calls Mary the mother of the faithful . . . The Pope goes farther' (*Chronique de la troisième session*, pp. 112–13).

127. 'It is our hope that . . . the Council . . . the place, the most excellent by far, which is due to the Mother of God in the Church . . . in such a way that we may honour her with the name *Mater Ecclesia . . .*'

128. Audience of 18 November 1964: 'The position Mary occupies is of a unique nature. She is a member of the Church, she too was bought back by Christ; she is our sister. But precisely because of her election as mother of the redeemer . . . and because she represents mankind perfectly and in a unique manner, she has every right to be called, in a moral and typical sense, the mother of all men, and especially ours, the mother of the redeemed and believing, mother of the Church, mother of the faithful'. And again, on 22 November, at the Angelus: 'Mother full of charity', to be venerated by 'all believers, all of us, not only as isolated individuals but also as a community'.

129. Laurentin, *op. cit.*, p. 40: *Mariam sanctissiman declaramus Matrem Ecclesiae, hoc est totius populi christiani, tam fidelium quam pastorum, qui eam Matrem amantissimam appellant.*

of it'.[130] In the period previous, only a few texts are *ad rem*. One of the very few is the following passage from St. Augustine's *De virginitate*: 'Mary is not the spiritual mother of our head: spiritually speaking, she will rather be said to have been born of him. But she really is the mother of us, his members'.[131] Antoine Wenger supplies us with another text, from the oldest account extant of the 'dormition' of Mary which he discoverd in a Syriac manuscript dating from the fifth century. Mary addresses Christ, the whole Christ, head and body: 'You are the Pleroma, I have given birth to you first of all and all those who hope in you'.[132]

It will be good, finally, to note that both Pope and Council have been equally at pains to remain in the direct line of patristic tradition (and Scripture too, of course) on the questions of the unique mediation of Christ and the unique worship of God. This is made clear, notably in n. 60, 64 and 67 of the Constitution, and of papal statements our example is a speech of 21 November 1964: 'Our particular wish is that the role of Mary, humble servant of our Lord, be clearly set forth as altogether relative to God's role and that of Christ, our only mediator and redeemer'.[133]

★

In conclusion, let us return to the 'typology'. The mystical analogy linking Mary and the Church is just as vividly appreciated in our age as it must have been in the time of Ambrose and Augustine. When, in its turn, the Second Vatican Council came

130. *In Apoc.*, 12, 14 (PL 17, 960). Cf. Bruno of Segin, *In psalm.*, 44, etc. Mary is 'Lady of all the Church' and 'daughter of the Church' (PL 164, 421a, 857–8; 165, 1021b).

131. *De virginitate*, ch. 6 (PL 40, 399).

132. 'In this text which alludes to Eph 4:13, Mary affirms her spiritual maternity of all who believe in her Son . . . The text, which has however no doctrinal pretentions, as good as states that Mary is mother of the Church': A. Wenger, *Chronique de la troisième session*, pp. 124–5.

133. A fruitful study might be made on the analysis of 'the teaching of Vatican II on the Virgin Mary' given by Mgr. Jorge Medina Estevez to Notre Dame's international theological congress in March 1966: *Vatican II, an Interfaith Appraisal* (ed. John H. Miller CSC, Notre Dame Press, 1967). See too Juan B. Alfaro SJ, 'Maria en el misterio de Christo y de la Iglesia segun el Concilio Vaticano II' in *Regina Mundi* (Rome 1966–1967), pp. 30–38.

to sketch it and outlined in a way that illuminated the doctrine on the Church as much as that on our Lady, its authority consecrated something that proceeds from the depths of Catholic consciousness. The learned, the historians of dogma and spirituality, have not been the only ones to examine the witness of tradition regarding these mysterious bonds.[134] This witness has been independently brought to light, and somehow re-invented and given new life by certain men deeply impregnated with the Catholic spirit, however much they might have differed in other areas.[135]

Hans Urs von Balthasar is one who often throws into relief what he calls 'the marian dimension'. He is at pains to show 'the mysterious continuity between the marian experience and the maternal experience of the Church'.[136] In *Le Coeur du Monde* he has Jesus say to the Church: 'Your face tends to become mysteriously identified with the face of my Virgin-Mother. She is the unique Woman, but in you she becomes the Mother of all . . .'[137] In his *La Prière contemplative* Mary, 'archetype of the Church', is considered at length as the archetype of Christian contemplation: 'the place of the incarnation of the word', she guards us against the danger of viewing the word as something exterior to us; it is after all, 'the most profound mystery at the centre of our being'. She warns us also, 'with consummate delicacy for our feelings', of the opposite pitfall: equating the word with our private inspirations. In Mary the faithful soul— 'the Church'—said the perfect 'yes' that is the origin and substance of all Christian contemplation.[138] In his *La Théologie de l'Histoire,* von Balthasar justifies this analogy with equal clarity

134. Bibliography in G. Philips, *Maria,* vol. 7, pp. 418–19.

135. For a Protestant witness: Max Thurian, *Marie, Mère du Seigneur, Figure de l'Église* (Les presses de Taizé, 1962). A confidential memoir sent in October 1959 to Pope John by Roger Schutz and Max Thurian contained this sentence: 'The interpretation of marian dogma in the sense of the relations between Mary and the Church, of which she is the type, may possibly facilitate the search for Christian unity'. Quoted by J. M. Paupert, *Taizé et l'Église de demain* (Fayard, Paris, 1967), p. 151.

136. *La Gloire et la Croix,* vol. 1, p. 357.

137. French edition (Desclée de Brouwer, Paris, 1956), p. 219.

138. French edition (Desclée de Brouwer, Paris, 1958), pp. 25–6, 73–4, 101–13, etc. See too *Herrlichkeit,* vol. 2 (Einsiedeln 1962), chapter on Dante (pp. 365–462).

and depth, showing its genesis in that real identity of Mary with 'the most intimate centre' of the Church:

In Mary, the creature, mother and spouse, the character of receptivity goes beyond that of a manifestation of the present divine plentitude. By this Mary becomes the original type of the Church. More than that, in the innermost core of her being, where she is really the immaculate spouse without wrinkle or blemish, the Church arrives at absolute identification with the mother and spouse of the Lord. For precisely this reason, the Church can have no essence on earth: her sense is all in Christ, hidden in God, and will appear only with Christ (Col 3:3-4) when the holy city will descend from heaven at the end of time (Apoc 21:2).[139]

With deliberately naive bluntness, Paul Claudel once declared to a correspondent: 'The holy Virgin Mary, so far as I am concerned, is the Church. I have never found any reason to distinguish between them'. What he meant by this of course was that in his mind the two realities were indissolubly united. Experience had taught him as much: on one Christmas Eve in the Cathedral of Notre Dame, while he listened to the Magnificat, all the faith of the Church burst through to him. From that moment he frequently returned to the ancient cathedral to pursue his 'theology course'. His teacher, he tells us, was 'the Holy Virgin herself and with what infinite patience and majesty!' 'Face glued to the choir-grille', he watched 'the Church live', and this spectacle, that leaves so many men inert and bored, was for him the way to complete understanding and new life. Because, he explains, 'what Paul told me and Augustine showed me, the bread Gregory broke with me with antiphon and response—there above me were the eyes of Mary explaining all'. The 'maternal and comforting majesty' that then enveloped him was at once that of the Church and of Mary. All he needed to do, without further distinction, was to rely on this

139. French edition (Plon, Paris, 1955), pp. 126–7. Cf. 'Truth and Life' (*Concilium*, 21, 1967): 'The Church, immaculate Spouse . . . to the extent that she is *already real,* and the nucleus and principle of belonging, is in Mary'. *Qui est chrétien?*, French edition (Salvator, Mulhouse, 1967), p. 71: 'Marie: l'Église'.

twofold and unique mother 'who confers silently in her heart and re-unites in a single focus all lines of contradiction'.[140]

We find the same lack of distinction, or rather, the same mysterious identification, in another writer. Though his spiritual orientation appears very different from the other two, a poem of Teilhard de Chardin will echo them closely. (We hope we evoke his name in this context with more justice than was sometimes the case at the Council.) Drafted in 1918, during the First World War, this poem describes the ascending stages of the 'Eternal Feminine' who speaking through the mouth of the biblical (and liturgical) wisdom addresses herself to men:

> *Ab initio creata sum . . .*
> *Et usque ad futurum saeculum non desinam . . .*

. . . God, I had drawn him towards myself long before you.

Long before man had measured the extent of my power, and divined the meaning of my attraction, the Lord had already wholly conceived me in his wisdom, and I had captured his heart.

Do you imagine that without my purity to seduce him he would ever have descended as flesh into the milieu of his creation?

Love alone is capable of moving a being.

God therefore, that he might find it possible to emerge from himself, had first of all to construct for his footsteps a road they would desire to walk upon, to spread all before him a perfume called beauty.

It was then he made me rise up, a luminous vapour, on the abyss—between earth and him—that he might come to live among you in me.

Do you understand now the secret of your emotion when you approach me?

. . . Placed between God and earth, as a region to which they are both attracted, I bring them together, passionately.

. . . And so it was in me that the meeting took place where

---

140. *L'Epée et le miroir*, pp. 198–203, etc. *Méditation sur l'Église* (2nd ed.), pp. 292–3 and 321–4. Cf. *L'Évangile d'Isaïe*, p. 212: 'The perfect moon, the faithful translator, is the Virgin Mary and also the Catholic Church'.

the birth and plentitude of Christ is consummated through the centuries.

I am the Church, spouse of Jesus.

I am the Virgin Mary, mother of all men.[141]

To this triple witness, we call another, l'Abbé Jules Monchanin. In some densely-packed sentences, Monchanin, in a meditation on the Virgin of the Indies, united the double typology that *Lumen Gentium* was to make its own, to another theme, also retained in the Constitution's seventh chapter, namely, the maternity of Mary in relation to the Church. He enlarges this theme, in the manner of Père Teilhard, almost into a kind of cosmic maternity:

Mary is the fullness of virgin and woman, of mother. A virgin always and *usque in saeculum,* everything virginal in the world before her announced her, and all virginity after her will be integrated in her. Is not the essence of virginity the unicity of its love? She is the perfect woman, receptive to God, fecund for and of God. Mother of the incarnated Word —her childbearing is comparable rather to the generation of the Word by the Father than to the childbearing of other women: *prius concepit mente . . .*—and so of the Church, of humanity, of the world: a cosmic mother, in fact, universal mediatrix, she who initiates renunciation and dispenses the joy that does not pass away; she who bears Christ and the Spirit, the Spirit who is in her gift, whose fullness she possesses and whose spouse she is, and the Christ to whom she continues to give birth, these two manifestations of the Father: she summons the Church to the secret of the Father . . .

She initiates and consummates, she is the reflection of the Principle, of the Mediator, of the Spirit. The Virgin of Israel, the daughter of Abraham will . . . revive contemplation of the Trinity. Prototype of the Church and its achievement, which is essentially the appeal to the Father whose paternity she temporally shares in, to the Son whom she brings forth

141. Teilhard de Chardin, *Écrits du temps de la guerre* (Grasset, Paris, 1965), p. 261. In *La vie cosmique* (1916) he said, again of Mary: 'Pearl of the cosmos, its contact point with the personal incarnated Absolute; the blessed Virgin Mary, Queen over all, true Demeter' (*op. cit.,* p. 48).

to *kenosis* and to growth, to the Spirit which, of her super-abundance, she communicates to creation.[142]

We should remark here that the bond between the Church and Mary is established, in Monchanin as in Teilhard, by applying to them the same wisdom symbol. And this too is, in part, a patristic resurgence: it represents the convergence of the two-fold application of the same sapiential texts in the Western liturgical tradition to Mary, and in the writings of the Eastern Fathers to the Church.[143]

When it privileged the theme of the people of God, the Council made the biblical image of the daughter of Sion more striking, in its double application to Mary and the Church. For, in the prophets the daughter of Sion personified 'the tiny, faithful remnant re-united at Jerusalem after the exile'. Now, for St. Luke Mary is this daughter of Sion; St. John and, after him, the primitive Church also saw her as 'the realization and personal expression of the Church that gives birth to the messianic people'.

Yet another point of convergence is the Apocalypse, in the twofold interpretation of the vision of the woman in labour and the vision of the new Jerusalem.[144] 'The woman who appears in the heavens and on the moon, among the stars . . . is first of all the Church, bringing forth the Messiah in tribulation, receiving the protection of God himself in the desert against the attacks of the dragon; but she is also Mary who represents this community of saints, the Church.'[145] As for the new Jerusalem, surely it is the Church herself who invites us to make this mystical identification when in her liturgy she extols the immaculate Virgin, applying to her the verse: 'I saw the holy city, the new Jerusalem, coming down out of heaven from God,

142. In *Dieu Vivant,* 3, 1945, pp. 47–8.

143. Cf. Louis Bouyer, *Le Trône de la Sagesse* (Ed. du Cerf, 1957), pp. 74–7 and 188–9. This however is a special aspect and does not find an echo in *Lumen Gentium.*

144. Cf. Pierre Benoit OP, *Passion et résurrection du Seigneur* (Ed. du Cerf, 1966), pp. 218–9. M. Le Déaut CSSP, 'Marie et l'Écriture' in *La Vierge Marie dans la constitution de l'Église, Bulletin de la Société française d'études mariales,* 1965.

145. Pierre Benoit, *loc. cit.*

made ready like a bride adorned for her husband.'[146] Does it not in some way teach us 'the pre-eminent personal realization of the Church in the Virgin'?[147] The recent teaching of the Council here only confirms, therefore, what the *lex orandi* had already suggested to us.

146. Apoc 21:2 Introit for the feast of the apparition of our Lady at Lourdes, 11 February.

147. L. Bouyer, *op. cit.*, p. 67.

4

The Pagan Religions
and the Fathers of the Church

I

The early Fathers of the Church declared very severely against the contemporary pagan cults. St. Paul had set them the example. He believed that if the gentile pleased God it was in spite of his religion.[1] Even when the Fathers thought they recognized features in these cults that seemed to have been borrowed from the Bible, they denounced them out of hand as the mark of the 'Monkey of God', who perverted truth and turned it into falsehood.[2] There is no point in dwelling on the details of their historically-conditioned judgments on concrete and particular facts. They did not apply them indiscriminately to all religions. In fact, it is only too obvious that the Fathers could not usefully speak of religious systems of which they were ignorant.

In general, it would appear they were better disposed to certain (though not all) of the philosophies of antiquity, especially 'Platonism'. Many of them recognized in the latter a light come from the Word that enlightens every man. Such was the view taken by St. Justin, for example, when outlining his teaching on the *'Logos spermatikos'*. (The actual expression derives at once from the gospels, Philo, and the Stoics.)

According to Justin, mankind before the Christian revelation received the seed of the Logos and so was capable of a partial understanding of the truth that would be fully manifest in Christ: 'The philosophers and legislators owe the just principles they have discovered to the fact that they have partially contemplated the Logos: thus does the teaching of Plato bear some resemblance to that of Christ, as does too that of others, stoics, poets, writers. But all of them expressed only a partial truth'.[3]

1. Cf. *L'Epître aux Romains* (traduction oecuménique, Paris, 1967), p. 37, note on 1:21: 'One sees the radically negative attitude of Paul towards the pagan religions. Their gross errors and excesses proved for him their culpability before the God of the gospels'.

2. Thus Tertullian and others.   3. *Second Apology*, ch. 10, n. 1–5.

Clement of Alexandria repeated the idea in the first of his *Stromata*: 'What I call philosophy is the sum of all the good that has been said in the schools and what we have been taught by laws accompanied by pious knowledge'.[4] Again, 'Philosophy is in some manner the work of divine providence'. Justin and Clement even went so far as to establish a parallel between the Greeks and the Jews, that is, between pagan philosophy and the Old Testament: 'The Lord', says Clement, 'distributed his gifts according to the aptitudes of each, Greeks and barbarians; to the one he gave law, to the others philosophy'.[5] By the illuminating action of the Logos, destined for incarnation, mankind came to know a certain number of essential truths that were in agreement with the Christian faith or could serve as a preparation for it. In paragraph sixteen of *Lumen Gentium,* and in paragraphs three and eleven of the Decree *Ad Gentes,* the Second Vatican Council made its own these patristic theories known collectively, since Eusebius of Caesarea, as the 'evangelical preparation'.[6]

Though he does not immerse himself in the polemical excesses of a Hermias or a Tatian—these remained the exceptions —Origen is, generally speaking, less conciliatory. He is especially sensitive to the fact that, in the thought of the Gentiles, 'all wisdom is tainted by blemishes'; nor does he forget that the philosophers (whose 'sophisms' he never tires of condemning) only too often conspire with idolatry in adoring the works of their brains just as others adore the works of their hands. But even Origen will allow a propaedeutic role to the better philosophies, for the building up of a Christian wisdom.[7] More

---

4. *Strom.*, bk. 1, ch. 7, 37, 6 (Mondésert and Caster, *Sources chrétiennes,* 30, p. 74); ch. 1, 18, 4 (p. 57).

5. *Strom.*, bk. 7, ch. 2. Cf. bk. 6, ch. 5: 'The one God has been known by the Greeks ethnically, by the Jews in a Jewish fashion, by the Christians spiritually'; and bk. 1, ch. 5, 28, 2–3 (SC 30, p. 65). Compare with St. Justin, *First Apology,* ch. 46, 2–5: 'All those who lived according to the Logos, in which all men partake, are Christians, even had they passed for atheists as, among the Greeks, Socrates, Heraclitus, and their like, and, among the barbarians, Abraham, Elias, and so many others'.

6. With references to Irenaeus, Clement, Eusebius. Cf. G. Martelet, *Les idées maîtresses de Vatican II,* pp. 42–50.

7. *In Levi.,* hom. 7, n. 6. *In Jesu Nave,* hom. 7, n. 1; *In Judi.,* hom. 2, n. 3; *In Jerem.,* hom. 16, n. 9; *Contra Celsum,* bk. 6, ch. 4, etc. Cf. Henri Crouzel, *Origène et la philosophie* (Aubier, Paris, 1962). See too Denis, *Epist.* 7, c. 2.

than he, St. Augustine was fond of seeing in Greek philosophy a harbinger of the Christian religion. And he was driven to this by the conviction—shared with others—that Plato had known 'Moses'.[8]

There is however a nice distinction to be observed here: if the Christian message is placed by Augustine (and Clement) 'before a background of universal religion', and universal religion is in this way presented as a kind of 'achievement', it is shown at the same time as a 'call to conversion: for all the partial logoi give themselves the status of absolutes and so form a culpable resistance movement to the true Logos'.[9]

On the other hand, Augustine frequently declares his very considerable reservations about those he calls Platonists (they are usually Plotinus and his followers). The invention of these doctrines, he explains, while in itself a good thing, has more than once resulted in atrophy of the soul caused by the pride they may engender. It matters little here that he was interpreting the 'Platonists' in the light of his own faith. They had every good reason, he says, for recognizing the existence of a word of God who is truth; they perceived 'in some manner, though distantly and with strained eyes'[10] the end of human life which is the vision of God, but the way to this vision they did not discover, since they did not know (or later would not recognize) the Word made flesh, Jesus, God in the humility of flesh. 'The perfectly valid philosophy' would have been inconceivable 'had not the sovereign God, moved by mercy for his people, inclined and lowered even to human form the authority of divine reason'. 'It is one thing, therefore, to look on the homeland from afar but quite another to find the path that alone leads there—and to adhere to this path'. Augustine is forever telling us this:

Truth itself, the God–Son of God, assuming humanity without losing divinity, has established this faith with a view to

8. *City of God*, bk. 8, ch. 11, etc. Werner Jaeger thinks that in indicating this prophetic role Augustine 'takes into account in an absolutely exact way that historical dimension which has recently come to light': *A la naissance de la théologie, essai sur les Présocratiques* (French edition, 1965, p. 56).

9. Hans Urs von Balthasar, *L'amour seul est digne de foi* (French edition, Aubier, Paris, 1966), pp. 13–14. See below, ch. 6.

10. *City of God*, bk. 10, ch. 29: 'In some fashion you see the homeland where you are to rest—though from a distance and at the end of a dust-blown road; but you do not keep to the road that leads there' (*Bibliothèque augustinienne*, 34, pp. 530–31).

opening to men the road that, by the Man–God, leads to the God of man. Here then is the mediator between God and men, the man Jesus Christ . . . Find the road and know your destination and you may hope to arrive. But if the road is lacking, what use is it to know the destination?[11]

Let us retain however this general truth from the thought of the Fathers, already expressed by St. Irenaeus: 'The Logos of God has never been absent from the race of men';[12] or St. Hilary's version: 'The light of the word will always shine where, simply, the windows of the soul are open'.[13] We find the same thought in Tertullian, expressed in a lapidary and often-quoted phrase (and one which was sometimes abused). In his *Apologeticus* Tertullian speaks of a 'naturally Christian soul' (*anima naturaliter Christiana*).[14] What he means by this he explains in his short treatise *Testimony of the Soul*: unsophisticated man bears spontaneous witness to the great fundamental truths of Christianity. These truths are those we now say pertain to 'natural theology'. Denied, obscured, or perverted, for the most part, by the pagan religions or by philosophical theories, the spontaneous movement of the soul affirms them. For all that, Tertullian does not claim that a man is born a Christian; he becomes one.[15] It would, consequently, be a travesty of his thought to assert that for him Christianity, or its equivalent, is to be found everywhere.

What appears from the thinking of the Fathers, taken very broadly as we have just done, is that if one may discover, either in the spontaneous movement of the human spirit or in the theories it has elaborated, preparations for welcoming the gospel, this can only be because all men are created for salvation; and it

---

11. *Contra Academicos*, bk. 3, ch. 19, n. 42. *Sermo* 141, n. 1 (PL 38, 776; cf. *Sermo* 117, c. 110, n. 16: PL 38, 670). *Confessions*, bk. 7, ch. 9, n. 13–15; ch. 21, n. 27. *De vera religione*, ch. 4, n. 7. *City of God*, bk. 11, ch. 2.

12. *Adversus haereses*, bk. 3, ch. 16, n. 1.

13. *Sur le psaume* 118, Lassued, 6 (ed. A. Zingerle, CSEL 22, 1891, p. 459).

14. *Apologeticus*, c. 17, n. 6 (ed. G. Rauschen, Bonn, 1906, p. 59). Cf. Minutius Felix, *Octavius*, c. 18, n. 11 (ed. Jean Beaujeu, Les Belles Lettres, Paris, 1964, pp, 27–8).

15. *De testimonio animae*, c. 1, n. 7: *Non es, quod sciam, christiana: fieri enim, non nasci solet (anima christiana)*. Cf. c. 5, n. 4: *Certe prior anima, quam littera; et prior sermo, quam liber; et prior sensus, quam stylus; et prior homo ipse, quam philosophus et poeta* (ed. C. Zibiletti, Turin, 1959, pp. 76 and 89). Cf. Origen, *In Rom.*, 2, 12–14 (bk. 2, n. 9; PG 14, 892b).

is the gospel that brings the gift and revelation of salvation to them. God's creation, as a result, entails consequences that the Fathers of the Church and the great medieval theologians had a more unified, more organic view of than later theology generally has had. God created man for a divine end. There must therefore be—however one is to explain it—something in man that prepares him for this end and for its revelation. One way of putting it would be to say, as Irenaeus, Origen, and others did, that God created man in his own image in view of their meeting.[16] Deep in human nature (and so in every man) the image of God is imprinted, that is, a quality that constitutes in it—and even without it—a kind of secret call to the object of the full and supernatural revelation brought by Christ.[17]

This doctrine is of vital importance. It offers a certain likeness to another patristic doctrine whose ambit is rather different but which we may mention in passing, a doctrine regarding the twofold relationship between man and the Word incarnate. While never receiving a definitive expression, this occurs very frequently in the writings of the Fathers. By his incarnation the Word assumed all human nature: *'naturam in se universae carnis adsumpsit'*, as St. Hilary has it more than once,[18] following Origen who had said in a phrase of even wider scope: *'Christus, cujus omne hominum genus, imo fortasse totius creaturae universitatis corpus est'*.

It follows immediately that every man, Christian or not, in the 'state of grace' or not, orientated towards God or not, whatever his knowledge or lack of it, has an organic link with Christ —and has it in such a way that he cannot lose it. But this primordial relationship is altogether different from that uniting the members of the 'mystical body' with their head. They alone are

16. In a similar manner St. Gregory of Nyssa distinguished two kinds of benefits accruing to man from God: some he has by 'participation', others are, properly speaking, 'gifts' (*The Creation of Man*, ch. 9; PG 44, 149b; SC 6, p. 114).

17. Cf. my *The Mystery of the Supernatural*. A similar doctrine in St. John of the Cross, *The Ascent of Mount Carmel*, bk. 2, ch. 4. The conciliar Decree *Ad Gentes*, on the missionary activity of the Church (7 December 1965), n. 7 *in fine*. It is true, as Karl Barth says, that the meeting between man and God is brought about by the word of God from on high; but it does not follow that there is nothing in the depths of man that awaits this word. Cf. Barth, *La proclamation de l'évangile* (1961).

18. *De Trinitate*, bk. 11, ch. 16: *Universitatis nostrae in se continens assumptione naturam; In Matt.*, 19, 5; *In psalm.* 51, 17, etc.

the beneficiaries of this union—this second relationship—who have received Christ and have made him welcome, in an explicit or implicit manner. In other words, by virtue of the assumption of all human nature by the Word incarnate, a primordial, essential and inalienable bond unites all men to Christ. This is what is sometimes called the 'inclusion' of all humanity in Christ. And it must be carefully distinguished from the mystical body. The mere fact of being man does not entail automatic membership in the latter.

This distinction is well enough summed up by saying that the first of these relationships, or the first of these two ways of belonging, is of the 'natural' order while the second is of the 'personal' order.[19] We remark the perfect conformity of such a doctrine with the christology of St. Paul for whom Christ is first of all present to all the cosmos created 'in him', and so to all men before being—as it were—the saviour of those who respond to his call.

II

What is the judgment of the Fathers on the religious phenomenon in its rapport with the Christian phenomenon? As we have said, their judgments on contemporary cults were very severe, not excluding even a Clement of Alexandria. But, as we have also said, these judgments are not normative for us: they were not pronounced on religions which the Fathers did not know. All the same, they did enunciate a principle of judgment which, to their minds, had a bearing on all non-Christian religions. This principle we must retain; it has normative value for us since it arises directly from the nature of the faith. In this case, the limitations of the Fathers' empirical knowledge alters not a whit its universal application.

The Church of Christ, they felt, had the duty from her faith in Christ to integrate (by converting) all the religious efforts of mankind. This integration envisages two basic ends: first, the purification, the opposition to and the elimination of the error

19. Again St. Hilary, *In psalm.* 121, 8: 'This Israel . . . is, from birth, taken up by the Lord because of the body, is saved if it believes in the cross, is glorified if it has confidence in the resurrection' (ed. Zingerle, CSEL 22, p. 575).

or evil inevitably present to a greater or lesser extent;[20] secondly, the task of assumption, assimilation, and finally transfiguration. One could take the prophet Ezekiel's vision of the desiccated bones as a symbol of this process: these scattered, emaciated members cannot be taken for a living being; only the Spirit, acting in the Church of Christ, is capable of effecting their passage from death to life.[21] Clement of Alexandria used a somewhat similar analogy. Pointing out the truths dispersed throughout the different schools of philosophy (and the heretical sects), he recalls the tragedy of Pentheus, his limbs torn apart and scattered by the Bacchantes: 'He who reassembles the scattered parts and restores to unity the perfection of the Logos, let him know that he shall safely see the Truth'.[22] Before him, St. Justin had said, in his second *Apology*: 'Our teaching surpasses all merely human teaching because in Christ we have the entire Logos'.[23]

Such a way of looking at things, associating unity and truth so intimately, is at once, we should note, very exclusive and very broad, very strict and remarkably all-embracing. The things we commonly say today about the integration of cultures—or 'values'—into the Christian faith were once said by the Fathers, often with considerable audacity, of the very religions themselves; they would have integrated all that might be salvaged from them and not just their 'cultural' elements—if indeed the religious and cultural elements of certain religions are susceptible of adequate distinction at all. They saw Christianity 'not as a limited confession, but as total, cosmic religion—as "*katholon*", in short—into which the partial elements were inserted when they had undergone the necessary purification. We see this process at work, for example, in the manner in which certain

20. 'Think of the disgusting "religious" literature of the Philistines and the Phoenicians which had such strong influence on the formal structure of the Psalms': Hans Urs von Balthasar, 'Parole et Histoire' in *Parole de Dieu en Jésus-Christ* (Casterman, Tournai, 1961), p. 259.

21. Newman used the same image in a similar sense in his *Parochial and Plain Sermons*, vol. 4, 11.

22. *Strom.*, bk. 1, 57, 6. Cf. André Méhat, *Études sur les Stromates de Clément d'Alexandrie* (Ed. du Seuil, Paris, 1966), p. 483. Hans Urs von Balthasar, *L'amour seul est digne de foi* (French edition, Aubier, Paris, 1966), pp. 13–14.

23. Ch. 10, 2–3.

pagan myths themselves were conserved as images of the Christian truth'.[24]

Consequently, we may say that the final judgment of the Fathers on the religious phenomenon, insofar as it can be deduced from the mass of documentation and the variety of attitudes, is a judgment of the dynamic order—if we may so call it. It is part of a theology of history. It is formulated as a function of the sole Church of Christ that bears the Absolute, Christ. Everything true and good in the world must, as St. Paul advises, be taken up into and integrated in the Christian synthesis where it undergoes transfiguration. The Fathers knew that even the anterior 'revelations' (cosmic revelations and those of Moses and Abraham) lapse and at the same time are accomplished in Christ. 'The entire redemptive plan found its expression, or was "incarnated", in the "grace" and "truth" which came to us through Jesus Christ and through the salvation that was not to be found elsewhere.'[25] All the more reason then for regarding other religions—whatever their merits—as 'salvific', that is, entering into or remaining in 'concurrence' with faith in Christ.

St. Augustine however, who in other respects may be classed as a rigorist, says that 'even the gentiles have their prophets'— but they were, he adds, prophets of Christ unknown to themselves. It was in the same sense that Clement of Alexandria said: 'God raised up from the bosom of Greece the most virtuous of its children that they might be prophets to their own people'. The thought of Augustine, Clement, and others is completed by a second assertion: 'In the Church of Christ alone does human kind remake and recreate itself'.[26]

In short, we have no business comparing diverse religious situations statically; nor should we institute comparisons between different religious systems in history with a view to either condemning them or admitting that this one or that may constitute a true 'economy of salvation' and have come from God

24. Hans Urs von Balthasar, *Dieu et l'homme d'aujourd'hui* (French edition, 1958), p. 192.

25. Jn 1:17; Hebr 4:12. Cf. Christopher Butler OSB, *The Idea of the Church* (Baltimore and London 1962): 'Exception having been made for divine revelations and dispensations which antedated the incarnation, the positive values of which have all been taken up into, and absorbed by, the Christian dispensation—so that none of them now has any standing in the supernatural order independently of Christianity—the Christian religious system is the only one that can truly claim to have divine authority and to embody God's saving purpose to mankind' (p. 151).

26. St. Augustine, *Epist.* 118, c. 5, n. 33 (PL 33, 448).

—whether one terms them 'ordinary' or 'extraordinary'. Even before a judgment was pronounced one way or the other, this would be to disjoint God's plan which bears the mark of unity. It would be to declare in favour of an *a priori* relativity in the very idea of religious truth. Putting different religions side by side is to admit the possibility that they all have equal claim—whatever they may be like—to be considered as of God. And yet they may propose not just different, but divergent, paths to be followed! They may even contradict one another on fundamentals! How, for instance, is the admission feasible that Islam, looked at objectively and as a whole, might be a divinely constituted way of salvation and that Buddhism might also be—when the former stoutly affirms monotheism and the latter comports with atheism?

But look at the problem from the opposite standpoint. If judgment is given as a function of Christ's Church in pilgrimage towards the Parousia, with an integrating and saving mission, then no longer can non-Christians be conceived of as independent units or, in other words, statically. All the good in them, we conclude, are such elements as may be integrated in Christ. Lastly, whatever is an objective means of salvation necessarily has a relationship with the Church. In every hypothesis, man's basic search, as witnessed by the religious phenomenon—even in its worst aberrations—must eventually find its true object in the revelation announced by the Church to the world. As for the grace that brings about the necessary conversion, it also comes, however tortuously, from the only Church of Christ, since it is through her that all men must be saved. God has wished to unite himself to humanity; the unique spouse is the Church. *Sola Ecclesiae gratia, qua redimimur.*[27]

In the Fathers, 'ecumenism', it has been said, 'is something dynamic, working ceaselessly to gain and transform the world according to the gospel'.[28] The important thing to note here is that the principle of this dynamism that must synthesize everything into its unique truth is not a mere concept or an arbitrary something-or-other. It is neither the 'idea of Christianity' nor 'Christianity' itself. It is a reality, an existence, an action, a

27. St. Ambrose, *In psalm.* 39, 11 (PL 14, 1061b).

28. G. Connan (Bucharest): *Le rôle des Pères dans l'élaboration de l'oecuménisme chrétien* (*Studia Patristica*, vol. 9, part 3a, Berlin, 1959, p. 157).

personal force: it is the very person of Jesus Christ. *Ego sum via, veritas et vita.*

Guided by the Fathers, we are always returning to this unicity of personal faith in Christ, the only saviour, who unites us to God in his Church. Whoever does not believe exclusively (in the sense already indicated) and without intellectual compromise in the truth of Christ is no longer a Christian. From this point on the effort of synthesis is doomed to failure.[29] But it is this unicity alone, let us assert straightaway, that brings about true universality. 'It seems at first the infinite richness of God contracts itself so as to concentrate in one place, the humanity of Jesus Christ, to the extent that in this unique Person "all the treasures of wisdom and divine knowledge are hidden" . . . Such an unheard of, inexorable, exclusive concentration of all the paths to God and all of man's relations with God in the unique mediator may appear to man as an incomprehensible violence done to his liberty, his dignity and quite heedless of the coming of age of the individual person . . . But in reality this unicity is universal and integrating and, for that very reason, catholic.'[30]

In a concrete, historical and collective conception of salvation such as we find, at least implicitly, in the Fathers, we are obliged to admit that 'universality is inconceivable in the absence of a unique event'. W. A. Visser't Hooft, analysing the thought of St. Paul in the Epistle to the Romans, reaches the same conclusion. From a slightly different point of departure, he eventually confirms what Hans Urs von Balthasar has said:

29. 'Faith in Christ is at the base of Christianity and adhering to it in faith is "conversion"; if one may speak of "bricks waiting" (to become part of a construction) these must pass into the furnace of the Spirit because they need a more radical transformation than a simple insertion into a new blueprint. As firewood before it is thrust into the fire, much of the human sap must be removed': Yves Raguin, 'Adaptation et conversation' in *Bulletin du cercle Saint-Jean-Baptiste,* 1965, pp. 325 and 327.

30. Hans Urs von Balthasar, *La prière contemplative* (French edition, Desclée de Brouwer, Paris, 1959), pp. 52–3. Again: 'Religion et culture chrétienne dans le monde actuel' in *Comprendre, revue de la société européenne de culture,* 17–18, Venice, 1957; also *Théologie de l'histoire* (French edition, Desclée de Brouwer, Paris, 1955), p. 167; *Foi et attente proche*: 'Every event with a bearing on salvation from the beginning to the end of the world happens on this most narrow path of all, this needle's eye: they happen in the bosom of divine intersubjectivity that was opened in Jesus Christ so that we might enter into it' (*Bulletin des Facultés catholiques de Lyon,* December 1966, p. 22).—Cf. Jacques–Albert Cuttat, *La rencontre des religions* (Aubier, Paris, 1957), p. 94: 'The traditionalists . . . deplore the exclusiveness of the Christian faith . . . without even suspecting that this apparent restriction is actually a gain in depth as in breadth', etc.

It might appear that the sole preoccupation of the New Testament is to coalesce everything into one point, one person, one historic event, so to produce an impressive synthesis of the innumerable human possibilities, to produce, in fact, an excessively narrow faith. But that is only one aspect of the question. The truth is, as Romans 5 demonstrates with all the clarity one might wish, that this narrow gate opens onto the vast horizon of an authentic universalism. The chapter that tells us of the unique revelation of Christ is also the chapter that speaks to us of all men. The attention he devotes to the unique saviour does not distract St. Paul from humanity. On the contrary, the preoccupation with the Unique leads inevitably to the consideration of all the others.[31]

There is, in fact, to labour the point, no question of comparing the merits of diverse religious systems, of confronting this one or that with some other which is thought more true, more perfect—which would be the Christian system. Rather it is a matter of thinking and believing that God has intervened in our history; that he has brought us the only principle capable of purifying us and uniting us to himself, namely, Jesus Christ, indissolubly 'he who reveals' and 'he who redeems'; further, that it is the Church, his spouse, who is his depositary with a mission to spread his good news; that it is in this way and none other that mankind will reach its destiny, gathered together into the 'mystical body'.[32]

There, in capsule form, is what the Fathers tell us. (*Christus*) *omnem novitatem attulit, semetipsum afferens.*[33] And indeed what other possible belief or opinion remains for one who has really given his faith to Jesus Christ?

Once this unicity of the Christ who reveals and saves is established in the heart, we can only regard with the greatest respect and, sometimes, the greatest admiration the discoveries sought after and, to some extent, found in the spiritual history of mankind, outside the revelation of Jesus Christ. 'The Church', Pius

---

31. *L'Église face au syncrétisme* (Geneva 1964), p. 131.

32. *Adversus haereses,* bk. 4, ch. 34, n. 1. Cf. Origen, *In Isaiam,* hom. 7, n. 5 (Baehrens, p. 285).

33. There is therefore no real univocity between 'the Christian religion and the other religions'. Which is not to say that Christianity is not also a religion.

XII said, 'gladly acknowledges the great and good realities that existed even before she did, even those outside her own domain'. The Pope was only giving voice to the constant tradition of the Church which we find expressed also in the letter of St. Agustine to the tribune and imperial notary, Flavius Marcellinus (to whom he also dedicated his great *City of God*): 'In the wealthy and famous Roman Empire God has shown the value of the civic virtues, even without the true religion, so that it may be understood when the former embraces the latter men will become citizens of another city, where the king is truth, the law is charity and the way of life is eternity'.[34]

There is, of course, no point in blinding ourselves to the waywardness of the myths, much less to the chaos and horrors that the developing history of the religious phenomenon reveals. But our reaction must not be a pure and simple rejection of this phenomenon in the light of the faith given to the true God, revealed in Jesus Christ. Neither Jesus himself nor his disciples practised such an inhumane dichotomy. The rejection of the false gods that man, by his still obscure consciousness or his perversity, persists in conceiving in his own image is not a rejection of human nature. Human nature was created by God and its religious aspiration must necessarily find expression or it will wither away. Also, from its very first appearance, Christianity has appeared to all (as formerly the cult of the God of Israel did) as a religion; indeed, on account of its extreme claims, as pretending to be *the* religion.

If one may say, in a correct but paradoxical formula, that Christ's death on the cross was the 'supreme act of religious "demythologization"',[35] this is not the equivalent of claiming that, all religion being myth, this death was the act by which all religion was repudiated: the more exact word is 'accomplished'. Then again, the more we see in past or contemporary societies elements of truth, beauty or goodness the more we must feel

34. *Epist.* 138, n. 17: *Deus enim sic ostendit in opulentissimo et praeclaro imperio Romanorum, quantum valerent civiles etiam sine religione virtutes, ut intellegeretur, hac addita, fieri homines cives alterius civitatis, cujus rex veritas, cujus lex caritas, cujus modus aeternitas* (PL 33, 533); quoted by Pius XII in his discourse to the Tenth International Congress of Historical Sciences, 2 September 1955 (*Documentation catholique*, 52, 1955, col. 1219–20).

35. Étienne Cornélis, *Valeurs chrétiennes des religions non chrétiennes* (Ed. du Cerf, Paris, 1965), p. 181.

that a place must be found for them—whatever their parentage
—in the Christian synthesis. But how is this to be achieved? No
one can say for certain till after the event. It is as impossible to
sketch the plan as it is to foresee the delays. Suffice it to hold to
our principle and put our confidence in the Holy Spirit. The
strength of the faith, the vitality of Christianity will realize the
miracle of conversion and integration, independently of theory.[36]
No more than faith does hope presuppose the full light of day.

III

The teaching of the Fathers is still vigorous today. We find it in
the teaching of the magisterium, notably in the encyclical
Evangelii praecones of Pius XII and in the texts of Vatican II.
Newman, who had been formed by the Fathers, initiated in the
last century a revival with rare beauty of expression and made
us admire the 'Catholic plenitude'.[37] So too, nearer to us in
time, did the Abbé Jules Monchanin in his long reflections on
the theology of the missions, arising from the encyclicals of
Benedict XIII and Pius XI. 'The Christian synthesis', he used to
say, 'which is mystery reflected in thought, is its own indicator
of reality: *index sui*. The plenitude both includes and rises above
partial truths, a conviction strengthened by each progress in
integration'. And applying this to India, he said:

> What Justin and Clement said of Greece may equally well
> be said of India. The Logos was mysteriously preparing the
> way for his coming and the Holy Spirit stimulated spiritually
> the gropings of the purest minds among the Greeks. The
> Logos and the Holy Spirit are again at work and in a similar
> manner in the depths of the Indian soul. Unfortunately,
> Indian philosophy is spotted with error and does not appear
> to have found its proper equilibrium. And neither did the
> Greek until the message of the risen Christ had been humbly
> received by Greece. Outside the unique revelation and the

36. 'The real work will be done, not by the theorists, but by the Holy Spirit who gives
the divine life to souls.' It should not be forgotten that 'it is often the element of truth
which these religions contain that at first impedes their embracing the full truth': Yves
Ratuin, *op. cit.*, pp. 322 and 328. Was it not in Judaism and hellenism that early
Christianity found its principal opponents?

37. *Critical and Historical Essays*, 12.

one Church, man everywhere and always is incapable of filtering the good through evil, truth through error. But once christianized, Greece rejected the errors of her ancestors —especially their too cosmic perspective and their forgetfulness of the transcendental aspect of the Absolute—and having been baptized in the blood of her martyrs, she became mistress of the world in philosophy, theology and mysticism. So, in the same manner, with confidence in the unwavering direction of the gospel, it is our hope that India, once baptized in the depth of her 'quest of Brahman' which has endured for centuries, will reject her pantheistic tendencies; and, discovering in the Holy Spirit the true mysticism, will engender, for the good of humanity and the Church, and for the glory of God, dazzling galaxies of saints and doctors.[38]

Hans Urs von Balthasar is thinking along the same lines when, showing a deep acquaintance with the Fathers but expressing also his own thought, he extols Christ 'the accomplishment of every element whose truth the religious myths of every people contain in part form'. But he denies that there is any question of finishing up with 'a fusion of Christ with Dionysus or Apollo' nor of 'making a cosmic religion of Christianity': for, if Christ and his Church have sole claim to the heritage of all that is truly human in the cultures and religions of all peoples, staking out this claim 'has, necessarily, a twofold aspect: it is achievement by judgment'.[39] This double aspect the Christian will do well to recognize, if he is not to do God an injury:

It would be ungrateful to the Creator to wish to present this power 'to transcend' (which is in man) as a simple absence of power, this form of contact with what is above the world as a *fabrica idolorum*; such a view leads necessarily to blasphemy. But one would be equally ungrateful to the author of grace and to the redemption not to see in the gift of grace an absolutely new and different reality which only consummates and completes the efforts of man because it first of all submits them to a transformation.[40]

38. Jules Monchanin, *Ermites du Saccidânanda* (Casterman, Tournai–Paris, 1956), ch. 1. See my *Images de l'abbé Monchanin* (Aubier, Paris, 1967).

39. *La Gloire et la Croix* (French edition, Aubier, Paris, 1965), pp. 420, 424, 429.

40. *Idem*, 'Trois signes du christianisme', appendix to *Théologie de l'histoire*, p. 167. Cf. H. van Stralen, *The Catholic Encounter with World Religions* (London 1966).

Yet another of our contemporaries, Father Teilhard de Chardin, also shows himself to be close to the thought of the Fathers. On the one hand, he casts an extremely critical eye over the details of the different human religions and spiritualities.[41] But, on the other, he appropriates for them the benefits of that law which applies to human achievement in every order, 'the law of integration of the natural into the supernatural'.[42] This integration, he tells us, is brought about by a process of 'segregation', 'convergence', 'transformation' and finally 'conversion'. Four words, four correlatives whose employment throughout his work would make an interesting study. He expresses the desire that Christianity, the divine and—properly speaking—revealed religion, might 'open its axes to embrace, in its totality, the new religious pulsation rising from below and asking to be made sublime'.

One may very well dispute his observations and judgments on this 'new pulsation'; but what is of importance here is that his wish is expressed because of his belief in the unique reality of the Word's incarnation[43] and in the 'unique power of divinization' placed by the Spirit of Christ only in his Church. This is what he again calls 'the unitive properties of the Christian phenomenon'. He realizes that 'without the Church, Christ evaporates or wastes away or annuls himself'; and in Rome he salutes that 'extraordinary focus of spiritual brightness', 'the Christ-pole of the Earth':[44]

41. Having said that 'the biological function of religion is to give a form to the free psychic energy of the world' and to lead 'to some supreme unification of the universe', he concludes: 'if we apply this double criterion to many kinds of religions, or even to secular moralities, which have succeeded one another *without interruption* in the course of history, the result is a shambles . . .' This does not however prevent his admiring certain elements, as the following lines, dated 19 June 1926 and written in Peking, witness (he is talking about a statuette of Kwannon): 'a little marvel of human and heavenly beauty . . . a true perfume of prayer . . . There is, outside the Church, a vast quantity of goodness and beauty which will only be perfected in Christ, no doubt. But in the meantime there it is, and we should sympathize with it if we wish to be fully Christian ourselves and if we want to assimilate it with God' (*Lettres de voyage,* Grasset, Paris, 1956, p. 91).

42. 'La Foi qui opère' (*Écrits du temps de la guerre,* Grasset, Paris, 1965), p. 325.

43. Cf. St. Irenaeus, *Adversus haereses,* bk. 3, ch. 16, n. 6: 'one only Christ, our Lord, coming all along the way of the universal economy, recapitulating all things in himself'.

44. *Ma position intellectuelle* (New York, April 1948), etc. Letter to M. T.–C., 7 October 1948. Other letters; on the 19th to his brother Joseph, on the 28th to the Abbé Breuil (*Nouvelles lettres de voyage,* Grasset, Paris, 1957), pp. 96–9. Cf. my *Teilhard missionnaire et apologiste* (Prière et Vie, Toulouse, 1966), pp. 49–51.

At the very heart of the social phenomenon, a kind of ultra-socialization is in progress: that by which the 'Church' forms itself little by little, unifying by its influence and assembling :-- their most sublime form all the spiritual energies of the no. phere;—the Church, the consciously Christ-absorbed portion of the world;—the Church, by super-charity the principal meeting-point of inter-human affinities;—the Church, central axis of the cosmic convergence and precise area of the excited meeting between the universe and Omega Point.[45]

Christianity, which Teilhard always envisaged in its strictly Catholic aspect, could also be compared to a 'phylum', that is, it lives and develops as 'a coherent and progressive system of spiritual elements collectively associated'. 'The experience exists to prove this, not only in law, but in fact.' It is in Christianity that 'the new attitudes' continue 'to form themselves by a perpetual movement of synthesis between the old credo and the newly-emerging insights of human consciousness and so prepare the way around us for the advent of a Christian humanism'.[46] While the crisis resulting from 'the renewal of the cosmic view that characterizes modern thought' is interpreted by some as an invitation, if not to abdicate their faith, at least to slacken it, to 'ease it off a little'—to the extent almost of depriving it of any substance—for Teilhard it meant drawing the opposite conclusion: 'from the very fact of the new dimensions taken on by the universe in our eyes, Christianity—through the living, organized axis of Roman Catholicism—is seen to be more inherently vigorous and almost more necessary to the world than ever before'.[47]

45. *Comment je crois* (1948), n. 24.

46. *Introduction à la vie chrétienne* (1944), n. 8. Cf. *Lumen Gentium*, n. 17: 'By her action, the Church brings it about that everything of good that is sown in the human heart and mind, in the rites and cultures of peoples, not only does not perish but is purified, uplifted and consummated, for the glory of God, the confusion of the devil and the happiness of mankind'.

47. *Le phénomène humain*, p. 330. Cf. *L'Esprit nouveau, Vers un renouveau chrétien* (*Oeuvres*, vol. 5, p. 122). When he speaks of a 'general convergence of religions on a Universal–Christ', Père Teilhard quite evidently does not therefore envisage this Christ–Universal as the product of a kind of pot-pourri of religions; rather, on the contrary, as the active, living and personal principle of the synthesis. See *Comment je crois* (1943).

Following Teilhard and Monchanin, and in agreement with the views of the English historian R. C. Zaehner,[48] Jacques-Albert Cuttat already discerns what he calls 'a spiritual, Christian renewal with the explicit aim of a catholicity so open in depth as to be able to draw all the mystical dimensions of humanity towards the unique, concrete universal', which is none other than Christ himself.[49] In his contribution towards this end he plots the course of a 'Christian assumption' of the Eastern spiritualities, outlines the conditions of convergence, shows how the universality of the Christian phenomenon is a function of its transcendence, since this phenomenon 'includes infinitely more than it excludes; or better still, upraises that which it would appear at first to exclude and radically reject'. He shows, too, how—unlike a hodge-podge syncretism—it unites and assumes to itself the 'non-Christian values' through 'processes of qualitative surpassment, conversion, transformation and recapitulation'. Needless to say, none of the 'combine-syntheses' history tells us of is perfect, nor *a fortiori* definitive; but the assimilatory power of the Christian phenomenon remains and every Christian conscience must persuade itself that this movement of assuming the non-Christian spirituality (and the subsequent processes) is something that begins at home.[50]

We may retain from the Teilhardian vocabulary the images of the 'pole' or the 'stem' or the 'phylum' or, once again, the 'axis'. Using these terms we shall sum up our argument in a simple question: does a single axis exist which if man follows he necessarily arrives at his final salvation, his union with God, thanks to the penetration of the gospel in the innermost core of men's hearts? Or are there several ways to salvation? Abandoning faith in this single, unique axis entails, as we have said, the

48. *The Convergent Mind: Towards a Dialectic of Religion* (Routledge and Kegan Paul, London, 1963).

49. Introduction to R. C. Zaehner, *Inde, Israël, Islam, Religions mystiques et révélations prophétiques* (Desclée de Brouwer, Paris, 1965), p. 35.

50. 'Experience chrétienne et spiritualité orientale' in André Ravier, *La mystique et les mystiques* (Desclée de Brouwer, Paris, 1965), pp. 825–1,095. What is said here about the pagan religions is explained about human values in Gustave Martelet SJ, 'Mystère du Christ et valeurs humaines' in *Nouvelle revue théologique*, 48, 1962, pp. 897–914. See also, by the same author: *Les idées maîtresses de Vatican II* (1967), pp. 103–30 (the Church, universal sacrament of salvation) and pp. 207–30 (Christ the recapitulator).

belief that the different religious systems, though in contradiction on essentials, of themselves bring salvation; that God has so wished it, that he has constituted them as such. It is very difficult to believe. We must have sufficient strength of mind to admit 'the basic incompatibility of certain doctrinal positions'.[51]

But there is more to it. Even if not formally contradicting one another, if several ways of salvation really exist, parallel in some manner, then we are faced with a great dispersal, not a spiritual convergence. And what we call—now inappropriately—'God's plan' is without unity. There must be an axis. Non-Christians have not yet located it. A Buddhist who does not concern himself with the march of history—who does not believe in such a thing—has no need, obviously, to search for an axis; there is no problem here for him. But if, as God's design would wish it, we care about man's salvation, if we believe that his history is something real, if we aspire to unity, then we have no choice but to search for an axis, a drawing and unifying force, which is the Spirit of the Lord animating the Church.

IV

We must, finally, answer a second question, or rather, a corollary of the first arising from the modern situation: did the teaching of Christ really bring something quite new to our earth?

Up to a certain point, even the non-believing historian, provided he is sensitive to spiritual things, must, we think answer: yes. As for the Christian, *his* affirmation cannot but be absolute. He observes everywhere in history the traces of the stumbling quest of man, created by God and religious by nature. He notes with admiration certain high points that could only have come about 'through the meeting of human experience with the universal action of God'.[52] But, at the same time, he knows that the Good News was proclaimed in a definite place and at a definite time. Man heard it and rallied to it. Its newness seemed obvious enough to him and when he came to think about it he decided that, in fact, the Word of God would scarcely have

51. Yves Raguin, *op. cit.*, p. 231.
52. *Ibid.*, p. 230.

4

taken the trouble to come and speak to us if he did not have something really substantially new to say.[53]

Between the two parts that may be distinguished in Jesus' work, that of the teacher and that of the saviour, that is, between revelation and redemption, as between the gospel and the Church, the intimate correlation seemed evident. It was the same man, Jesus, who taught and died. And in this double role he showed that he was also more than man: the being who sacrifices himself for all is also he who demands unconditional adherence to his teaching and person. What is the meaning of this joint aspect?

If God had wished to save us without our having anything to do with it, the sacrifice of Christ would have alone sufficed. But does not the very existence of the saviour presuppose that a long collaboration had already been an established fact? Besides, such a salvation would be unworthy of the kind of persons God has wished us to be. In any event, God had no desire to merely salvage humanity like a wrecked ship: he wanted to put life in it, his own life . . . Whence it is that humanity must actively cooperate in its own salvation. To the action of his sacrifice Christ has joined the objective revelation of his Person and the founding of his Church. Revelation and redemption are linked . . .[54]

There can now be no possibility, therefore, of separating in principle these two aspects of the unique mystery of salvation. Any more than one may assert that salvation comes solely from Christ and yet suppose that as an *a priori* possibility this salvation might by-pass the teaching of Christ. There is, for mankind, no 'salvation without the gospel'. Furthermore, in its faith in the sole mediator, Christian tradition has never distinguished between him through whom interior grace comes and him by whom objective light comes. (Though, as we shall see, both aspects might find themselves disassociated in a comparison of

53. See, in much the same sense, André Manaranche sj, *L'homme dans son univers* (Ed. ouvrières, Paris, 1966), p. 52: 'The Good News would be a mere useless accessory!' And Dominique Bertrand, 'Dieu donne sa Parole à son peuple' in *Christus*, 53, 1967, p. 38: 'If we have nothing really new to say, what is the point in talking at all?'

54. *Catholicisme*, new edition (1965), p. 143.

their different ends.)[55] Just as there is one redemption, there is but one revelation, and the charge of communicating both the one and the other has been laid on one Church.[56]

If our observation is exact, then some consequences follow with a direct bearing on certain present-day discussion that may have arisen through a misunderstanding. That the grace of Christ is active outside the visible Church, her teaching and her sacraments, has always been recognized; though it has, regrettably, suffered occasional eclipse. The famous axiom *'extra Ecclesiam nulla salus'* did not bear the same general sense when it was first enunciated by the Fathers as many today appear to think.[57] It applied to certain very concrete situations, to the cases of those responsible for schism, revolt or betrayal.[58] That 'anonymous Christians' will be found in diverse milieux where, one way or another, the light of the gospel has penetrated, no Christian could possibly still deny. Even that he might find it elsewhere, by virtue of some secret operation of the Spirit of Christ, this also may be admitted. In any case no one has the right to declare the grace of the redemption his own personal prerogative.

To hold, however, because this is so, for an 'anonymous Christianity' spread throughout the world, would not be logical, though it might sound so. Neither would it be logical to conclude, as is still done, to an 'implicit Christianity' which it would be the sole concern of apostolic preaching to render explicit— still essentially unchanged. All of which would be as much as to say that the revelation we owe to Christ was no more than the

55. See for example St. Augustine, *The City of God*, bk. 11, ch. 2 and 3. Like it or not, the separation we speak of here deprives the gospel of any point.

56. Jacques Dournes criticizes, in *Spiritus*, 24, 1965, p. 261, the theory that sees in any religion whatever a 'possible way of salvation' and the 'accommodating formula' according to which the role of the missionary 'would nowadays be a conduct pagans from the implicit to the explicit'. As Fr. Jossua has remarked in *Revue des sciences philosophiques et théologiques*, 1965, p. 597: 'the sense of the absolute beginning of individual conversion and of the originality of Christianity is too overwhelming' to allow such a theory to gain much support.

57. Thus Gregory Baum in *Concilium*, 21, 1967. Cf. *Catholicisme*, pp. 148–50. Cyprian, *De unitate Ecclesiae*, c. 6 (PL 4, 503–4). Cf. Lactantius, *Div. Inst.*, bk. 4, ch. 30 (PL 6, 543a).

58. It is in this authentic sense that Dietrich Bonhoeffer uses the axiom in his *Gesammelte Schriften*, vol. 2, p. 238 (cited in René Marlé, *Dietrich Bonhoeffer*, Casterman, 1967, p. 65).

surfacing of something that had always existed.[59] When a St. Augustine, for instance, saw the grace of Christ operating in the holy men of Israel who, consequently, 'before the incarnation already belonged to the economy of grace and not that of the law',[60] he did not confuse the two economies as if the Old Testament, considered in history, already in its time possessed all the reality of the New. How much the less can one regard pagan humanity, in its self-created cults, as 'a Church unaware of itself'!

Such a position, it seems to us, to be tenable at all would have to begin by joining two problems—problems it is essential to keep rigidly apart from the outset! First, the problem of truth and the efficacy for salvation of a given religious doctrine and organism; secondly, the problem of an individual's achievement of salvation made universally possible by virtue of divine grace, traditionally treated in the Church as 'the problem of the salvation of infidels'.[61] This would also lead ipso facto to the neglect of the actual history of mankind, to the setting up c ome *a priori* notions as guidelines—notions that suppose that here is in practice no difference between religions, that they have a common relationship, that they may all equally play the role of 'means' or 'ways of salvation'.[62] And this, in the last analysis, is to say that they share an aptitude to raise themselves up into a kind of 'transcendental unity'[63]—if it is not more accurate to say

59. There is a new criticism of this expression in J. Dournes, 'Lecture de la déclaration par un missionnaire d'Asie' in *Vatican II, Déclaration sur les religions non chrétiennes* (Ed. du Cerf, Paris, 1967), pp. 84–112.

60. *De peccatorum meritis et remissione*, bk. 2, ch. 10–11 (PL 44, 116).

61. The distinction between these two problems or 'perspectives' is made by Jean Daniélou commenting on Hebr 11:6 in *Bulletin du cercle Saint-Jean-Baptiste*, April 1965.

62. The proverb given in answer to the Franciscan Guillaume de Rubroucq by the great Khan Monkut is well known: 'As God has given several fingers to the hand, so he has given several ways by which men may reach him'. Cf. the intervention of Most Rev. Fr. Guéguiner, October 1965, during the debate on the Decree concerning the missionary activity of the Church: 'The current opinion that all religions are efficacious and adequate means of salvation, and the theory of the "tiny remnant" Church, destroy the teaching of the gospel. This opinion deprives the plan of God of its content and ruins the *raison d'être* of the Church'. Cf. *Documentation catholique*, 19 December 1965, col. 2169–74.

63. This is a traditional thesis, illustrated by the work of Fr. Schuon entitled *L'Unité transcendentale des religions*, and criticized by J.–A. Cuttat in *La rencontre des religions* (Aubier, Paris, 1957), especially pp. 81–7; p. 96: 'The Christ who would not be the unique revelation would not be the Christ'.

that they achieve this through their common insignificance.

It is amazing to see the extent to which certain writers—who in other respects give ample proof of their profundity of thought and spiritual quality—seem to lose their heads when they come to examine religious history and the spiritual development of humanity. Putting the matter more generally, in these times of ours when mankind is becoming conscious of its unity, when so many people are coming to realize that they are involved in a historical situation, when a truly definitive doctrine of the last things is being reborn in the Church, one cannot but be astonished to remark among the specialists in the problem of salvation a momentary forgetfulness of these essential truths and their insistence on an individual outlook.

Such a theory, finally, would suppose—to be precise about it —that the truly 'revolutionary' newness of the Christian contribution would be misunderstood. (This is what seems to us most serious though we attribute the holding of it to no one.) The Christian contribution must not be evaluated, obviously, in the clearly weakened and often even unnatural manner in which each of us assimilates it. The theory would appear to be ignorant not only of the idea but of the very reality of this 'metanoia' brought about by the gospel which has profoundly transformed the 'heart' of man and even his consciousness. In other words, it would seem to forget—if we may be allowed to use this anachronism—the highly *existential* character of the Christian revelation. If one were to credit the explanations of it sometimes put forward, it would appear to be practically reduced to the teaching of some formulas, without inner penetraion, without renewal force. It would be a kind of exercise in etiquette, a decoration attached to the outer shape, leaving untouched the inner form of things which it had always had— though in an 'anonymous' manner. In short, all it would be good for would be to serve as an identification of an existing reality; and it would be difficult to see 'why some men would continue to bear the title of "Christian" since their claim to possess it "anonymously" could be so easily justified'.[64]

Let us repeat that all we have done here is draw to its logical conclusion a contemporary tendency whose exaggerated forms

64. Hans Urs von Balthasar, *Bilan* 1965.

may sometimes be corrected immediately, since their contradictions become apparent. A fevered search is in progress and we realize, of course, that the ideal equilibrium will not be attained at first. There will be general agreement, however, we have no doubt, that the thesis we have discussed and criticized does not correspond, in its most sweeping form, to the idea of revelation presented to us by the recent Constitution *Die Verbum.* Nor does it correspond to the sentiments of a St. Paul, ideally placed to know, when, recalling that he had been 'seized' by Christ, he wrote to his beloved Galatians: 'It has pleased God to reveal his Son in me'.[65] And if we must say with the author of the Epistle to the Hebrews that the covenant concluded in Jesus Christ has made 'void' the Mosaic,[66] how much the more must we agree that in relation to this 'new covenant' all natural religions, all spiritual situations previous to this event are void!

Again, when Paul wrote to the Philippians: 'Keep in yourselves the thoughts and sentiments of Christ Jesus',[67] can anyone seriously believe that all he was offering was a little banal advice about something already practised and lived for years and years, apart from the small detail that the men of those times did not yet know the name 'Christ Jesus'? Is it really necessary to have deeply meditated on the Cross, must one be more than a weak and mediocre Christian to recognize some, at least, of the wholly new light that Christ has spread all over the world?

In Jesus, there has appeared to us not only someone who reveals to man what man already was but also 'through the perfect illumination of the Light'[68] from God someone who, revealing the depths of God, changes man radically. In other words, the overtly Christian revelation cannot be reduced to an expression of the revelation of consciousness that is reflexive, positive, made historically objective (and therefore, doubtless, relative and passing). By the incarnation of the Word, God

65. Gal 1:15–16; cf. Rom 7:17. See *Catholicisme*, pp. 222–3. 'St. Paul tells us that Christ is the commencement of a new humanity, and that the upsurge of humanity in Jesus Christ is an event comparable to the original creation of the world and of man': Jean Daniélou, *Mythes païennes, mystère chrétien* (Fayard, Paris, 1966), p. 74.

66. Hebr 8:13.

67. Phil 2:5.

68. St. Gregory of Nyssa, *In cant.*, hom. 5 (PG 44, 864cd); and on the new creation of the Church: 'It is the apparition of new skies and the new earth, it is the transformation of man, renewed in the image of his creator by a superior birth' (44, 1049bc).

approaches man in quite a different way still from the voice of conscience and the objective Word that resounded on our earth twenty centuries ago did not consist in a simple—and sterile—elucidation. It is quite true that as regards the individual the important thing is not the ideas he professes about religion, but neither was—and this is the point—the revelation of the incarnate Word made to bring just 'ideas': it is 'inseparable from a personal, creative communication to the highest degree'.[69] It is, as Dietrich Bonhoeffer said, 'the recreation of existence'.[70]

No less clear than that of Scripture on this subject is the thought of the Fathers of the Church, those pre-eminent witnesses of the Christian novelty. As we have seen, an Irenaeus insists at length on the secret action and the illuminations of the Logos all through history. For all that, he vigorously underlines the novelty of Christ: 'We would have had no way of knowing the things of God had not our master become man while remaining the Logos'.[71] Christ, he says again, brought with him that innovatory principle foretold by the prophets which 'was to renew and revitalize humanity'; and once having really 'contemplated his face, heard his words and enjoyed his gifts, the man of sense will not ask "what more have you brought"?' Any more than did the men who preceded and announced him.[72] This is to affirm the indissoluble union between revelation and salvation in Christ.

The same thought finds expression again in our days in some arresting phrases of Teilhard de Chardin. Reflecting on the Christian concept of revelation, he sees that there is a fundamental relationship between the substance of dogma and the faith of the believer:

One day, by the voice of the prophets or of his Son, God makes his influence explicit. He manifests himself as living, personal—one and triune at the same time. *Fides ex auditu.* At this moment, if the soul is faithful, its desires—hitherto

69. Louis Bouyer, *Dictionnaire théologique* (Desclée de Brouwer, Tournai, 1963), p. 494. Cf. John XXIII, *Humanae salutis,* 25 December 1961, on 'the eternal, vivifying and divine energies of the gospel'.

70. *Nachfolge* (Munich, 6th ed., 1958), p. 17.

71. '... for no other tells us of the things of the Father unless it be his own Word' (*Adversus haereses,* bk. 5, ch. 50 (PG 7, 1120).

72. *Adversus haereses,* bk. 4, ch. 34, n. 1).

confused—*encorpify* around the new truth . . . Almost shape-less (a simple invitation to uplift) in the pagan soul, the *sensible* attraction of Christ is enriched little by little in the Christian. Gradually he models himself on the articles of the creed since these fall from an inspired mouth into hearts that are docile.

Revelation creates *a man's spirit in the measure that it illuminates that spirit . . .*[73]

To conclude, let us repeat that such thoughts where we seem to meet and join, at a basic level, all believers in Christ, do not exclude the possibility of salvation, through the operation of the grace of Christ, for any man.[74] As it appears from the teaching of St. Irenaeus, if a man accomplishes the divine will for him in the history of salvation then this man will have his place in the perfect achievement. Esteem and admiration are not ruled out for the efforts to search and create made by the natural religions and spiritualities we read about.[75] How, for example, 'can we fail to admire the loftiness of the Buddhist ideal; the concern of the hearers to detach themselves from the passions and the perishable world; the vow of the Bodhisattva to consecrate themselves to the welfare and happiness of all beings; the purity of moral standards and Buddhist discipline; the efficacity of the methods proposed for the calming of thought and so many other features as well?' (Mgr. Etienne Lamotte)

'Each religion bears traces of light which must not be disdained or quenched; every religion raises us towards the transcendence of the Being without which there is no reason for existence, for thinking, for responsible work, for hope without illusion. Every religion is a dawning of faith and we await its full daybreak.'[76] If we know how to make ourselves attentive to the Good News which has come to us and if it occupies a really vital place in our hearts; if it arouses in us a spirit of admiration comparable to that which, as we see from history, characterized so many true Christians of every generation; if it remains for us what it was so clearly for them and, in fact, is—truth

74. Cf. St. Augustine, *De div. quaest.*, q. 44: 'Aliud est enim, etc.'

75. Cf. my book *Aspects du bouddhisme* (Ed. du Seuil, Paris, 1951), pp. 8 and 53. See also *Amida* (Paris, 1955) on the Japanese cult of Amida and the spiritual life of the Amadist: ch. 12, pp. 287–307.

76. Paul VI, Easter message, 1964.

itself and the innovation, the unique 'saving Word'[77]—then, recalling also that the Word-made-flesh is equally he who enlightens all men, we shall learn how to discern everywhere, even where still in darkness, even where sullied, this 'dawn of faith'. We shall learn to appreciate its value and to understand its irreplacable role in the divine plan for mankind's salvation. As for such theories as cannot be fully reconciled with either the words of the saviour himself or the consistent attitude of his followers, we shall not be beguiled by them.

A missionary has recently recalled for us the true doctrine, in terms that sum up both the tradition of the Fathers and the teaching of the Council. If the Çhristian's mission, says Father Jacques Dournes, is really to bring the news of Christ to men, thereby revealing to them 'what they essentially are', then the invitation is not to maintain the status quo but to open themselves to the influence of him who alone can fulfil their deepest wish. The Christian's mission is to teach them what they must become, to present them with 'the essential innovation' of this unique 'Event': Jesus Christ. The turning to Christ is not a simple 'realization of an already existing reality': it inevitably entails 'a rupture, a radical change of position, the efficacious sign of beginning in the mystery of Christ'. This is why 'however deep his respect and tender feeling for the human values of non-Christians, the Christian cannot but wish on them that wrench that is indispensible for renewal and so achievement, real plenitude'.[78]

But the individual responsibility of announcing and witnessing leaves to the theory an element of secrecy.

APPENDIX

A similar problem to the one we have been raising set Maurice Blondel and the Abbé Johannes Wehrle at loggerheads for a while in 1904. It was actually the same problem but its statement

---

77. Acts 12:26. This is what Jean Daniélou calls 'the radical distinction between religions and revelation' (*op. cit.*, p. 72).

78. 'Lecture de la déclaration . . .', *loc. cit.* Cf. Karl Rahner, *Mystique terrestre et mystique chrétienne de l'avenir* (1961): 'Christianity . . . is the herald of an entirely new, entirely other, dimension of human existence . . . God has *assaulted* this world so constituted. He offers to its anxious search an issue in his own infinity' (in *Mission et grâce*, vol. 3, pp. 149 and 150). Teilhard de Chardin, *Le Phénomène humain*, p. 329: Christianity expresses itself 'by the appearance of a specifically new state of consciousness'.

is at first somewhat confused. It was less a question of two really opposing theses than of two tendencies, or points of view. The occasionally dogmatic assertions of the points of view, however, divided the two friends.

On 28 July Wehrle wrote to Blondel. In his efforts to bring out the following paradox he hardened the stand of the latter: 'Can we usefully construct the notion of a Christ who would not have been a revealer, who would have contented himself with dying in a corner for us not caring that anyone should know about it?' Again, the next day, more temperately: '(You exaggerate a little) when you rely on the conscience of Christ to take responsibility for the reneging of our own. Not that your view is not perfectly true in itself; but follow up your argument and you will find yourself forced to lessen the part played by knowledge in religion and having—correctly—insisted on the necessity of Christ's conscience you will see how the necessity of human conscience is disproportionately played down'.

In a memoir of 12 August, Wehrle explained himself more positively: 'By revelation (I understand) the sum of those supernatural manifestations of God to humanity considered as a collective body . . . It appears to me dangerous to say that "revelation simply outlines the conditions necessary for salvation". I believe, on the contrary, that revelation itself is the first of these conditions. I refuse to see in it only a reality chartering our salvation course: I believe I must . . . see in it a reality that effects salvation insofar as it is achieved in collective humanity by the power and merits of the redeeming Christ . . . In my eyes, revelation is not the simple manifestation of what is, but the efficient cause of what ought to be. It is therefore, in the most positive and active sense of the word, salvific . . . I see great danger in placing revelation on the one side and redemption on the other, as though they were objectively independent realities . . . Considered in Christ (they) are indissolubly united through the principle of their inspiration and their fully conscious finality. Jesus gives and reveals himself in virtue of the same supernatural love of his creatures. He plans to save and redeem them as much by his teaching as by his sufferings . . . In giving himself for us he is revealed and in revealing himself he gives himself to us'.

94

As for Maurice Blondel, he answered on 18 August: '. . . I also believe in the consubstantiality of Being and Thought, and so in the essential, final solidarity in the matter of salvation, of the redemption and revelation'. And on the same day, in a letter to M. Fernand Mourret (who played a kind of umpire's role in the argument): '(I had no wish) to indicate that revealed knowledge is not the efficient cause of what ought to be: for I believe that, on the contrary, revelation is the active and original cause of salvation; and speaking of what it manifests as a condition of salvation I understood that revelation itself is primarily manifest as such . . . I have never claimed that it is merely a blueprint for salvation, like a simple Platonic contentment'.

A little later Blondel wrote to the young Augustin Leger who was interested in the problems then arising from Loisyism and whose over-subjective views were tending to lead him astray: '. . . If the objective knowledge of supernatural truth and the social authority of the visible Church is not absolutely indispensable for individual salvation, they remain, for all that, positive realities, substantially true and good, destined to be known and believed and obeyed, ontologically necessary to the redemption of all—even those profit from it under certain subjective conditions, without knowing its realization in history . . . Catholicism would no longer be what it claims it is if, disowning the usefulness of revealed knowledge and the concrete reality of the supernatural and redemptive order, it ended up in that individualism and equivalentism to which certain of your formulas seem to point'.

The story of this discussion and many of the letters on the subject exchanged by Wehrle, Blondel and Mourret will be found in the work of René Marlé sj entitled *Au coeur de la crise moderniste, le dossier inédit d'une controverse* (Aubier, Paris, 1960), ch. 7, pp. 225-96. Cf. M. Blondel, *Histoire et dogme* (1904), p. 65.

5

Paul VI, Pilgrim to Jerusalem

Inside St. Peter's, on Wednesday, 5 December 1963, while the final touches were being put to the modest schema on 'the instruments of social communication', a rumour began to circulate among the Fathers who were stretching their legs in the long naves of the basilica or in the corridors of the sacristy: the Pope would shortly announce something extraordinary, he would speak of a forthcoming pilgrimage to Jerusalem . . . The news spread through the benches in the aula, up to the tribunes, but the thing seemed unreal; no one dared believe it. Presently, however, when all were back in their places, the Holy Father began to read his speech for the closing of the session. His words were followed in the photo-copied texts that had been distributed at the entrance; they dealt entirely with the Council. Having reached the end and speaking above the first sounds of applause the Pope said that he had something to add. Immediately an attentive silence fell. Then, taking up a new sheet of paper, in a strong voice mixed with emotion and firmness, Paul VI spoke:

> We are so profoundly persuaded that for a happy issue to the Council prayer and good works are so essential that we have decided, after mature deliberation and much prayer, to go on pilgrimage ourselves to the land of Jesus, our Lord. In fact, with the help of God, we intend to travel to Palestine next month (January) to meditate in the holy places where Christ was born, lived, died, and ascended into heaven, the first mysteries of our faith: the incarnation and the redemption. We shall visit that venerable land from which Peter came and to which not one of his successors has returned.
>
> We shall return there for a short period as a humble expression of prayer, penitence and spiritual renewal to offer Christ his Church, to call our separated brothers to this one holy Church, to beg divine mercy on behalf of peace among

men, in these times so clearly precarious, and, finally, to beseech Christ our Lord for the salvation of the entire human race.

May the blessed Virgin Mary guide our steps; may the Apostles Peter and Paul and all the saints look kindly from heaven on our venture! We ask you, too, Venerable Brothers, to accompany us with your prayers so that you may be present to our mind and for the happy conclusion of this Council to the glory of Christ and the good of the Church.

Some words of cordial thanks followed, addressed to the Observers, Auditors, and all who had worked for the Council. Then the moving remembrance of bishops 'absent and in sorrow' and lastly the customary apostolic blessing.

As he spoke, the Holy Father's emotion communicated itself visibly to all. Had everyone immediately grasped the importance of the announcement? All, at any rate, were somehow gripped and, to judge by the applause that suddenly burst forth, even if the audience had not analysed their feelings in depth, all were conscious that an historical decision had been made. A great hope was born.

Since that morning of 5 December each day brought fresh news of the details of the coming pilgrimage. Theories were put forward, imaginations fed on the ever-broadening perspectives. Marvellous dreams were dreamt and were given full rein. As with every sensational development the newspaper commentators studied the possibilities of the occasion from every angle, and all the consequences likely to ensue. An ingenious parallel was worked out between the visit of John XXIII to Loreto and that of Paul VI to Jerusalem. Both Pius XII and John, it was said, had wished to go to Lourdes. It was pointed out that Paul would be the first Pope to leave Italy in half a century, and so on and so forth.

There was hope that this visit of the Sovereign Pontiff to the Holy Land—given the Pope's declared conditions for making it —would contribute in some measure to efface in the Moslem mind the sad legacy of the crusades. His crossing of the frontiers between Jordan and Israel would serve, it was also hoped, as a prophetic sign of the much-desired peace between the Arab world and the Israelis. But, quite properly, the ecumenical aspect of the papal initiative received most attention: it was, in fact, reasonable to suppose that its potential for achieving union was greater than any amount of writing or discussion. What more appaling scandal could there be for a Christian than the sight of the endless disputes, as savage as they are wicked, between the different Christian confessions in the very land where Christ lived and died? What better sign could there be, what sign more eloquent to effect reconciliation, than a prayer for unity recited in these very places by a Pope of Rome, enthusiastically welcomed by all, in spiritual—and maybe, as some suggested, visible—union with the representatives of the other Christian churches.

To me it seems that up to now the deepest import of the gesture has not been generally appreciated. The wholly interior principal import which does in reality warrant our high hopes but which remains even if these hopes will not be altogether realized, this, it appears to me, has not been discerned, though it also may be seen from the words of the Pope's announcement. No doubt it has been felt obscurely, otherwise the enthusiasm of the Christian world could not be adequately explained. But there will be no harm in an attempt to make it more explicit.

There is a close link between the opening speech of the Pope at the second session and his closing speech at the same session. This hints at a patiently pursued design on the part of Paul VI. In the first of these speeches, it will be recalled, a long paragraph was devoted to the extolling of Christ, 'our principle, our way, our hope and our end'. The Council was adjured never to forget the link that unites 'the holy and living Church which we are' to Christ 'from whom we came, by whom we live, to whom we are going'. On this assembly, he pleaded, 'let no other light shine than that of Christ, the light of the world: let no other truth retain our interest save the words of the Lord, our only Master'. Borrowing the words of the liturgy he cried: 'It is you alone, O Christ, that we know; it is to you with simple and pure heart we pray in our sorrow. Listen to the cry of our supplications!' In what he said then we can recognize the first expression, still obscure and symbolic, of what he would later state clearly in the closing speech:

While our prayer is rising to heaven we seem to see Christ

98

himself, present to our ravished and astonished eyes, as the majestic Pantocrator of your basilicas, my brothers of the Eastern Churches, and also those of the West. In the splendid mosaic in the basilica of St. Paul Outside the Walls for instance, we see ourselves in the person of the humbly adoring figure or our predessessor, Honorius III, who, tiny and prostrate, kisses the feet of the immense Christ who dominates and blesses with kingly majesty the assembled congregation, that is, the Church. This scene, it seems to us, is reproduced here and not as a picture or a painting but as a historical and human reality which acknowledges in Christ the source of redemption and of his Church, and in the Church his emanation and continuation, as it were, at once terrestrial and mysterious. It is as if the vision in the Apocalypse were being painted before our eyes: 'He showed me the river of the water of life, sparkling like crystal, flowing from the throne of God and the Lamb' (Apoc 22:1).

There is between the speeches more than just continuity. The gesture announced in the course of the second gives full weight to the words of the first, while these convey the full sense of the gesture. If we may rightly expect glorious results from the Pope's pilgrimage, for Christian unity and world peace, these are not the primary or even the principal reasons why the gesture, however unexpected, is admirably opportune in the present situation: it is, first of all, a gesture of faith, *the* essential gesture to make the full signification of the Church appear. If it is true that the twentieth century may be called 'the century of the Church' and that therefore the Second Vatican Council should be, in fact, 'the Council of the Church', no more expressive gesture could have been found than the sight of the Church going, in the person of her visible head, to prostrate herself at the feet of her Lord. By this pilgrimage the entire Church, 'tiny and as it were prostrate', prepares to go and kiss the feet of Christ. She returns to her birthplace, though not to revive a nostalgic memory; at the time when she is commemorating the events that led to our salvation, she acclaims in him, 'who by dying destroyed our death and by rising again restored our life', also him who never ceases to be 'the hope of humanity, our only sovereign master, pastor, bread of life, our priest and victim, unique mediator between God and men, saviour of the earth, future king of the eternal centuries'.

All Christians may expect to benefit from this simple pilgrimage, this gesture 'of prayer and penitence', because no other gesture could in so striking a fashion not only recall them to their origins but also invite them to re-attach themselves to the very centre, the heart of their Christian faith.[1]

In the course of these last centuries we have more than once heard the reproach directed at our Church, in the person of her representatives, that she has become self-complacent, that she is only all too willing to regard herself as the centre of things, that she speaks of herself as though she were the first beginning and the final end of everything. In short, she has been accused— and these are the very words that have been used—of putting herself in the place of God, of indulging in self-idolatry. The accusation is monstrously excessive, but it cannot be denied certain appearances could have given grounds for it.

In delineating the doctrine of the mystical Body, for instance, the mystical identity of Christ and the Church was sometimes so conceived as to accentuate the distinction between the head and the members, the better to deal with the subordinate relationship of the latter to the former. And then preachers too often have recourse to an over-insistence and especially over-exclusiveness in 'faith in the Church'. The expression may, of course, be interpreted in an excellent sense; but it is also open to abuse and we should not forget that in tradition it is reserved for faith in *God,* following the normative example of the Apostles' Creed.[2] And there was the 'triumphalism' denounced by one of the Fathers during the first session. This reveals itself

1. The press and television had, as we know, a field day with all the details of the pilgrimage—and there was no harm at all in it. Though we would say that in reporting such things the picturesque and the 'human interest' material tends to dominate, and so the matters of real significance are consigned to small print. What was amazing, however, was that afterwards several commentators thought it well to criticize the transformation of what had been originally announced as a gesture of humility into a noisy and public spectacle. The gesture was all it set out to be, the faithful were delighted to be able to follow its various stages, and if one believes that there was an occasional noisy indiscretion it is not fair to blame it on those who would have drawn other criticisms on themselves if they had tried to moderate the zeal of the correspondents.

2. It is regrettable that this doctrinal nuance which was for long taught as something essential, and which today serves to corroborate the first chapter of the conciliar Constitution *Dei Verbum,* should nonetheless be disappearing from the normal language of the French Church.

in a certain style of adornment and manner of speaking which can still be found here and there. Has it not happened, even in quite recent times, that well-intentioned orators and preachers who in other respects said much that was wise, felt compelled to conclude their speeches with a declaration that all they said was said 'for the greater glory of the Church'—as if beyond the Church's glory there was none worth considering?

Paul vi's gesture has overthrown all that. By its own logic it is such as to remedy all these defects, to dispel all this forgetfulness. It was John xxiii's wish that the present Council prepare the way for a future council of union, leading on from the Church's aggiornamento. The present Pope is showing us what the desired aggiornamento really means, what is needed to make it really decisive. If, as he said in a speech to the Curia, the aggiornamento must be the perfecting of all the visible and invisible aspects of the Church, then all effort which neglects the inner realization of perfection is quite useless. Before becoming effective in institutions or even in manners, the aggiornamento must win its battle with inner realities: the minds and hearts of men and their attitudes towards the faith. In Christianity the gesture of faith is all-commanding. And it is precisely a gesture of faith that Pope Paul made in his pilgrimage 'of prayer, penitence and spiritual renewal' to the places where Christ was born, lived, died, and rose again. In the Pope's person the Church proclaims that she is the Church of Jesus Christ and does not wish to be anything else. Far from making herself the centre, she refers everything to Christ. She 'prostrates' herself to kiss the feet of Christ.

Among the major reforms envisaged in the programme of aggiornamento there is much talk today of some kind of decentralization. Without denying the considerable interest of such a proposal for a new vitality in the body of the Church, there is something that appears to us infinitely more important: a 'decentration', to coin a phrase, which is doubtless always in progress in the Church under the influence of the Spirit of Christ, but which makes only imperfect progress in the members of the Church. This spiritual 'decentration' is all too rare among them, though through it is revealed the most profound nature of the Church'. The arrival of the Pope in the Holy Land as a 'humble worshipper' made it evident to all and once more summoned men to its practice.

The symbolic richness and the usefulness of the papal gesture is practically inexhaustible. All Christians, and those in particular who felt obliged to make those criticisms of the Catholic Church which we have been talking about, can today be very happy. We may all together share in a great hope. No, the Church is not seeking her own glory but that of her Lord only. In the long pilgrimage from the earthly to the eternal Jerusalem, she wishes to follow 'humbly' in his steps, conforming herself to him in example as in word. If she calls all men it is only to lead them to him, communicating to them the salvation that comes from him alone.

6

A Witness of Christ
in the Church:
Hans Urs von Balthasar

As Ludwig Kaufmann has justly remarked in a recent issue of
Orientierung, it is disconcerting that from the first summons of
the Council by John XXIII it did not seem to have occurred to
anyone to invite Hans Urs von Balthasar to contribute to its
preparatory work. Disconcerting and—not to put a tooth in it—
humiliating, but a fact that must be humbly accepted. Perhaps,
all in all, it was better that he should be allowed to devote himself completely to his task, to the continuation of a work so
immense in size and depth that the contemporary Church has
seen nothing comparable. For a long time to come the entire
Church is going to profit from it.

Indispensable though such things undoubtedly are, Hans Urs
von Balthasar is not a man for commissions, discussions, compromise formulas or collective drafts. But the conciliar texts
that resulted from them—of Vatican II and of all previous
Councils—constitute a treasure that will not be yielded up at
a single stroke: the Councils are the work of the Spirit, and so
these texts contain more than their humble compilers were
conscious of putting in them. When later the time comes to
exploit this treasure it will be seen that for the accomplishing
of this task no work will be as helpful and full of resource as
that of von Balthasar.

One thing we see immediately: there is not one of the subjects
tackled by Vatican II that does not find a treatment in depth—
and in the same spirit and sense as the Council—in his work.
Revelation, Church, ecumenism, priesthood, liturgy of the
word and eucharistic liturgy occupy a considerable portion.
Valuable insights on dialogue, on the signs of the times and the
instruments of social communications will also be found . . .
Before the Fathers of the Council had insisted that the dominant
role of Christ be recognized in the schemas on the Church and

revelation, von Balthasar had seen the need. His voice was an advance echo, as it were, of the voices that were raised in St. Peter's to ask for an adequate statement of the role of the Holy Spirit. The Virgin Mary in the mystery of the Church, its prototype and anticipated consummation, is one of his favoured contemplations. Gently, but with all the force of love, he has denounced those eternal temptations of churchmen, 'power' and 'triumph', and has at the same time recalled to all the necessity of witnessing through 'service'.

His spiritual diagnosis of our civilization is the most penetrating to be found. Though it would be going too far to claim that he had produced a complete outline of the famous Schema 13, he did, certainly, anticipate its spirit when he shows how 'in the same way that the Spirit calls the world to enter into the Church, so he calls the Church to give herself to the world'; and he warns us that no good will come of a facile synthesis of the two. In many cases one would also find in his writings the means to avoid the pitfalls of false interpretation which inevitably follow upon a call to aggiornamento.[1] And if, finally, one is seeking (always in line with the Council) the doctrinal framework needed before beginning the dialogue with the non-Christian religions and the various forms of modern atheism, one can safely go to von Balthasar.

His work is, as we have said, immense. So varied is it, so complex, usually so undidactic, so wide-ranging through different genres, that its unity is difficult to grasp, at least at first blush. But, strangely enough, once you have got to grips with it the unity stands out so forcefully that you despair of outlining it without betraying it. It is like a radiant impulse penetrating from a central point to all corners of his work. With the astonished perception of the immense culture he enjoys, displayed without pedantry, must go equal appreciation of the strong judgment that dominates this culture. The reader has to appreciate the breadth of thought that is never narrow or doctrinaire even when it had to be (or believed it had to be) hard and trenchant; and yet, at the same time the reader has to feel the rigorous balance of doctrine that is, in both senses of the

1. We should state straightaway that he has courageously declared war on certain wild abandons that are a betrayal of the Council. Had more allies rushed to his flag, he would have had no need to write certain rather savage pages.

word, profoundly catholic. And our problem does not end there: the reader must also be brought to see that he is never confronted with a purely theoretical construction; nor is von Balthasar a polisher of systems. Author of thirty books, some of them very long, neither is he a book-factory! Every word he writes envisages an action, a decision. He has not the slightest time for 'that certain economy of the mind which budgets and spares itself': everything is squandered that the 'personal meeting' with God may be arrived at without delay.

★

This man is perhaps the most cultivated of his time. If there is a Christian culture, then here it is! Classical antiquity, the great European literatures, the metaphysical tradition, the history of religions, the diverse exploratory adventures of contemporary man and, above all, the sacred sciences, St. Thomas, St. Bonaventure, patrology (all of it)—not to speak just now of the Bible —none of them that is not welcomed and made vital by this great mind. Writers and poets, mystics and philosophers, old and new, Christians of all persuasions—all are called on to make their particular contribution. All these are necessary for his final accomplishment, to a greater glory of God, the Catholic symphony.

Many of his books are historical studies or translations or anthologies: he likes to remain in the background of the pictures he commissions to serve as witnesses of the truth of man or of God. He was twenty-five when he published his first work, *The Apocalypse of the German Soul,* which was a historical commentary on the whole of German thought. A new edition has since appeared. Another book was an anthology of Nietzsche. He has written commentaries on the Epistles of St. Paul to the Thessalonians and the pastoral Epistles. He has published his own translations of many of the Fathers: Irenaeus, the Apologists, Origen, Gregory of Nyssa, Augustine. To several he has devoted a special study that in each case gave new life to its subject: *Presence and Thought,* for instance, on Gregory of Nyssa; *Cosmic Liturgy* on Maximus the Confessor. He has given us a commentary on part of Augustine's *De Genesi ad litteram,* and

105

also on part of the *Summa Theologica* (Questions on Prophecy). His translations include the revelations of St. Mechtilde of Hefta, the Spiritual Exercises of St. Ignatius (whose devoted disciple he is) the *Carnets Intimes* of Maurice Blondel—as well as the greater part of Calderon's religious drama. His incomparable translation of the lyric poems and *Le Soulier de Satin* of Claudel are well known.

He had done critical studies on Martin Buber and R. Schneider, on Péguy and Bernanos (*Le Chrétien Bernanos* was one of the last books the Abbé Monchanin read in the summer of 1957 at Kodaikanal). The substance of a book (recently reprinted) which is a confrontation of the Protestant Reformation and Catholicism he owes to his close contacts with a neighbour in Basle, Karl Barth. He has discussed the message of the two French Carmelites, Elizabeth of the Trinity and Thérèse of Lisieux. The second volume of the monumental work he was long engaged on, *Herrlichkeit,* consists of a series of twelve monographs in which Denis and Anselm meet Dante and John of the Cross, Pascal and Hamann meet Soloviev and Hopkins . . .

Without ever abdicating his freedom to criticize, he is at ease with all, even those whose genius might appear most foreign to his own; but when the time comes to disagree with them he does not hesitate. He excels at highlighting the original contribution of each. He admires human wisdom wherever he finds it—but surpasses it. Sensitive to man's *Angst*, he emerges from it in faith. The light from so many ancient sources allows him to illuminate the present situation and the accumulated wisdom of the centuries allows him, if we may be permitted the metaphor, to bury his arrows ever deeper in our present reality.

The inner universe he introduces us to is thereby, in its marvellous variety, perfectly unified. As in Tolstoy's epic, a broad and calm atmosphere prevails; as in Dostoievsky, this atmosphere is electric with sharp spiritual insight. All is patterned around a lofty and unchanging notion of truth, outlined in his beautiful work *The Phenomenology of Truth*. Truth is the cornerstone on which his theology of history is erected, more particularly in two essays. Finally, every word is designed to set in relief a basic anthropology relating to modern situations and the most pressing problems being faced by man today.

The contribution of the positive sciences is, perhaps, rather neglected, though scientific knowledge is assigned its proper place. The arts, it seems to Balthasar, have more to offer by way of illuminating suggestion. He realizes, in fact, that the great works of art—and every great work is a work of art—go beyond purely esthetic categories so-called and ought to be accepted, as they were conceived of by their artists, as efforts to complete a full image of man. Elsewhere he remarks that since the Renaissance man is no longer thought of and understood in the cosmological context but in an openly anthropological one. And since 'in an anthropological era the highest objectivity can only be attained by total engagement on man's part', we see the heightened dramatic character of all modern thought worthy of the name, a character that corresponds to the drama of existence itself.

Emerged from the cosmic development that nursed him, no longer in any way capable of regarding himself as one object among many, no longer having any home but his own fragility, man, Balthasar thinks, is more predestined than ever 'to become religious man' if he is to surmount this crisis of 'dereliction' resulting from the new situation. His rapport with God acquires a sudden urgency; the biblical teaching of man made in God's image becomes better delineated in his eyes and without the stage of natural knowledge being destroyed in the process the revelation of Jesus Christ presents itself to him more than ever as the necessary response to the interrogation forever carried on by his being. In his existence in time and history that constitutes 'the visible explication of the existence-form of the God-Trinity', Jesus comes to reveal this unknown that was in him to man; then 'his features expand, are enlightened and deepened when he meets, not a mirror giving him back his own image, but his own supreme original'.

★

It is quite impossible to resume here the theological thought of Balthasar; we shall confine ourselves to the essentials. What distinguishes it and gives it its most striking originality is its refusal to be labelled. It can neither be termed old nor modern; it derives from no school and repudiates all piecemeal 'specialization'. With no axe to grind, no single aspect of a given question is stressed to the detriment of the others, or rather, it refuses to delay over successive 'aspects' while never forgetting to consider each. The indispensable technicalities are there, whether in criticism (certain work on Origen, Evagrius or Maximus, for instance, is inspired guesswork followed up by the most rigorous verification), or in dialectic (as in the dialectic 'of the unveiling and enveloping' to different degrees of revelation, or in the relation of negative natural theology to the knowledge of the 'face of revelation' which is given to us in Christ). But, for all that, it retains a highly synthetic character which breaks down the barriers to the interior life of things where the classic theology of our times is usually bogged down. While it does not offer direct pedagogical models his thought—and even the form of his thought—may be usefully meditated on in view of the new directions which Christian thought must take since the Council.

Not to labour the point, let us say that in a word his theology, like our ordinary credos, is essentially trinitarian. Not that the Trinity fragments the divine unity—it is revealed to us, after all, through its work of salvation which is itself perfectly one. The 'seamless coat' and the 'lance's thrust' are the symbols he uses to bring this home to us: 'A mystery that is broken up into aspects (*epinoiai*) will yield its secrets to the enquiring intelligence. But there is one mystery that absolutely refuses to do so, the irreducible mystery of the *persona ineffabilis*. From him the whole Church comes in his death, with the water and the blood—the Church which with all its truths, liturgies and dogmas is only an emanation of the heart that broke unto death, as Origen better than anyone else understood'. For the 'thrust of the lance on Golgotha is in some manner the sacrament of the spiritual thrust that wounds the Word and so spreads it everywhere . . . The Word of God cast into our world is the fruit of this unique wound.'

It is the Holy Spirit who ceaselessly introduces the Christian into the heart of this mystery. The Spirit's role is to 'refresh daily the memory of the Church and to supplement it in a renewed manner' with all truth. It is he who realizes everything in the Church and in her individual members 'as it was he who formerly realized the incarnation of the Word in the womb of the Virgin'. Also Balthasar likes to point out the continuity between 'the marian experience' and 'the maternal experience of the Church'. He likes to speak of 'the marian dimension of the Church' or of 'the marian Church', and this simple expression we take as a condensation of his teaching which might also be said to be the teaching of the Church, or of the Virgin Mary, or of the Spirit, or of Christ, or of the Christian life.

His refusal of all biased 'modernity' is by no means a refuge from present problems and the responsibilities they impose. The theologian must transmit a truth which is not his own and which he must guard against alteration, but transmitting this truth and watching over change to new situations demands from him a real involvement: 'One sees this very clearly in the manner in which St. Paul transmits what had been confided to him. Anyone who would wish to insert himself without danger in the chain of tradition and transmit the treasures of theology almost as children who switch their hot buns from hand to hand in the hope of not being burnt would be the victim of a sorry illusion, quite simply because thoughts are not buns, or rather because from the morning of Easter combat was joined between the material and the spiritual.'

This theology, so traditional, remains relevant today and indeed does not lack a certain audacity. Balthasar has recalled to the modern theologian the immense task that confronts him and that even demands that he give all his attention for the moment to the central core of the doctrinal question: 'The doctrines of the Trinity, of the Man–God, of redemption, of the cross and the resurrection, of predestination and eschatology, are literally bristling with problems which no one raises, which everyone gingerly sidesteps. They deserve more respect. The thought of preceding generations even when incorporated in conciliar definitions is never a resting-place where the thought of the following generations can lie idle. Definitions are less the end than the beginning . . . No doubt anything that was won after a severe battle will be lost again for the Church, which does not however dispense the theologian from setting to work immediately again. Whatever is transmitted without a new personal effort, an effort which must start *ab ovo*, from the revealed source itself, spoils like the manna. And the longer the interruption of living tradition caused by a simply mechanical transmission the more difficult the renewed tackling of the task.'

The boldness of such a programme, we can see clearly enough, does not lead us onto perilous or uncharted seas; it does lead us to the living centre of the mystery. Its primary concern is for completeness. Balthasar's audacity is not an irresponsible appetite for novelty: it proceeds from a faith whose daring grows in proportion to the strength of its roots. He himself is one of those men of whom he has spoken, men who devoted the work of their lives 'to the splendour of theology—theology, that devouring fire between two nights, two abysses: adoration and obedience'. The denials and lack of comprehension of our age disconcert few people as little as him. Fashionable opinion does not intimidate him; he never entertains the temptation to water down the vigorous affirmation of doctrine or the rigorous demands of the gospel.

There is no trace in him of that terrible inferiority complex rampant today in certain milieux among many Christian consciences. The Church, he has written, following St. Jerome and Newman, 'like the rod of Aaron, devours the magicians' serpents'; and by her, at the same time, he says in an image borrowed from Claudel and which might also be described as Teilhardian, 'the key of the Christian vault is come to open the pagan forest'. And so Balthasar has done. With calm assurance he displays to all, as far as he can, the entire Christian treasure. He does not hesitate to oppose, not criticism nor psychology nor technology nor mysticism, but all their unwarranted pretensions, and no one can accuse him of blaspheming what he does not know.

He knows the value of 'human sciences', he admires their conquests but will not submit to their totalitarian claims. His many observations on scriptural exegesis, on the need for a spiritual intelligence and, in particular, on the blindness of a certain historico-critical method of dealing with the meaning of the history of Israel and the person of Jesus, all deserve a wider audience. 'The Holy Spirit', he writes, 'is a reality which the philologists and philosophers of comparative religion are ignorant of or at least "provisionally put into parentheses".' Balthasar removes the parentheses, or rather, he shows us how the Holy Spirit himself removes them.

Some of his criticisms—they are rare—might appear harsh. In every case they arose from his concern not to compromise in essentials. He is too far above pettiness, too heedless of passing modes and allurements—particularly those that arise from pseudo-science or a frivolous faith—not to find himself often isolated. In the end however his attitude is always positive. His 'tough line' is the same as that he has pointed out in Christ, the revealer of love. He is being true to his own position when he warns us of the dangers of isolationism. He does not wish 'through enthusiasm for the glorious past of the Church', or for any other reason, that the Christian 'forsake the men of today and to-morrow. Quite the contrary. It is the duty of all who represent Jesus Christ—be they bishops or layfolk—to keep open their perspective on the human; never to allow any manoeuvre to push them back into isolationism or negative attitudes.'

★

'We live in a time of spiritual aridity.' The vital equilibrium between action and contemplation has been lost, to the apparent profit of the first but, for the very same reason, to its detriment. Balthasar has tried to re-establish this equilibrium. All his work has a contemplative dimension and it is this above all that gives it its profundity and flavour.

He introduced again into theology the category of the beauti-ful. But make no mistake, this is not to say that he surrendered the content of the faith to current notions in secular esthetics.[2] He began by restoring to the beautiful its position as a tran-scendental—this beauty 'which demands courage and decision at least as much as truth and goodness, and which may not be separated from its sisters without drawing upon it their mys-terious vengeance'. He has not agreed with those theologians who based their work on the separation of esthetics from theology. His 'theological esthetics', however, is not an 'esthe-tic theology'; it has nothing to do with any estheticism what-ever. Moreover, in this mystery of the beautiful which men, not daring to believe in it, converted into a mere appearance, he sees, as in the biblical description of wisdom, the union of the 'intangible brilliance' and the 'determined form', which re-quires and conditions in the believer the unity of faith and vision.

2. He had already said in *Le Chrétien Bernanos*: 'There exists a theological, an ecclesio-logical esthetic that has nothing at all to do with estheticism. In it pure human beauty meets with the beauty of the supernatural.'

The beautiful is at once 'image' and 'strength', and is so par excellence in that perfect 'figure of revelation' who is the Man-God. Faith contemplates this figure and its contemplation is prayer. Balthasar has observed that wherever the very greatest works were produced there was invariably 'an environment of prayer and contemplation'. The law is verified in an analogous manner even in the pagan domain. 'The proud spirits who never prayed and who today pass for torchbearers of culture vanish, with regularity, after a few years and are replaced by others. Those who pray are torn by the populace that does not pray, like Orpheus torn by the Maenads, but even in their lacerations their song is still heard everywhere; and if, because of their ill use by the multitude, they seem to lose their influence, they remain hidden in a protected place where, in the fullness of time, they will be found once again by men of prayer.'

Jesus, 'indivisible Man-God', is at once the object and model of Christian contemplation. This is the burden of the great work, still uncompleted, *Herrlichkeit*. (The first volume has recently appeared in a French translation under the title *La Gloire et la Croix*.) The idea is put into action in a book like *The Heart of the World* in which the heart of Jesus opens to us in a kind of lyrical explosion. It may be seen even better perhaps in *Contemplative Prayer,* an introduction to prayer that is at the same time a complete—the most complete available—outline of the Christian mystery. We shall restrict ourselves here to quoting just one passage, a passage of great value in that it provokes reflection on the primordial importance of contemplation in the life of the apostle:

All we have been able to attest to other men, our brothers, of the divine reality comes from contemplation; of Jesus Christ, of our Church. One cannot hope to announce in a lasting and effective manner the contemplation of Christ and the Church if one does not oneself participate in them. No more than a man who has never loved is capable of speaking usefully of love. Even the smallest problem in the world will not be solved by one who has not met this world; no Christian will be an effective apostle if he does not announce, firm as the 'rock' Peter, what he has seen and heard: 'We did not bring you the knowledge of the power and advent of our Lord

Jesus Christ on the warrant of human fables, but because we
have been privileged to see his majesty. He received from God
the Father honour and glory . . . This voice (of the Father)
we have heard when we were with him on the holy moun-
tain . . .!'

And he continues, not without sadness:

> But who today speaks of Thabor in the programmes of
> Catholic action? And who speaks of seeing, hearing or touch-
> ing that which all the zeal in the world cannot preach and
> propagate if the apostle himself has not recognized and ex-
> perienced it? Who speaks of the ineffable peace of eternity
> beyond the conflicts of earth? But also, who speaks of the
> weakness and obvious powerlessness of crucified Love whose
> 'annihilation' to the extent of becoming 'sin' and 'accursed'
> has given birth to all strength and salvation for the Church
> and mankind? Whoever has not experienced this mystery
> through contemplation will never be able to speak of it, or
> even act according to it, without a feeling of embarrassment
> and a twinge of conscience, unless, indeed, the very naivety
> of such a basically worldly business has not already made this
> bad conscience apparent to him.[3]

On specifically Christian contemplation Balthasar's judgment
is equally lucid: 'All the other unfathomable depths to which
man's contemplation may penetrate, when they are not ex-
pressly or implicitly the depths of the trinitarian, human–divine
or ecclesial life, are either not real depths at all or are those of the
devil'. There is a kind of spiritual pride that is the most dangerous
inversion of all; many so-called 'mystical' states are no more
than 'artificial paradises' and as for those 'sublime spirits' who
search for the way apart from or above the humanity of the
saviour, 'what they experience in their ecstasies is the disguised
ghost of their empty nostalgia'. Even in the Christian spiritual
life it may be opportune to recall that 'the gospel and the Church
are not dionysiac: their overall impression is of sobriety; elation
is left for the sects'.

3. He has also, most opportunely, pointed out the danger of a 'liturgical movement'
which would be 'isolated and uncontemplative', just as he has also indicated his 'con-
tempt' for a 'war that has been declared against the contemplative tendency and that is
sometimes waged in the name of eschatology'.

These reservations do not, however, tend in the slightest to 'crush the Spirit'. The Spirit must be received in the manner in which he gives himself, in a sort of tension between precision and enthusiasm: 'The saints knew how to do it: it is precisely this precision of the image of Jesus as projected by the Spirit that they would wax enthusiastic about; and then their very enthusiasm, expressed with precision, would convey to all the fact that they had been gripped by this image. Even if they were full of indubitable truths that might express for all the world the truth of the gospel, the saints were not arid text books: expressing the truth was the very life of the saints gripped by the Holy Spirit of Christ.' Even for the humblest and weakest Christian it is in the simplicity of his *yes* of acceptance and openness, in imitation of the *yes* said by Mary to the Word, that the element of contemplation, inserted at the base of every act of faith by the Holy Spirit, is developed.

★

No matter what subject he is treating, and even if he never mentions any of their names, it is very clear that Balthasar was formed in the school of the Fathers of the Church. With many of them he is on more than familiar terms: he has in many ways become almost like them. For all that, he is no slavish admirer: he recognizes the weaknesses of each and the inevitable limitations that result from the age in which each lived. With his customary frankness he criticizes even those he admires and loves most. But their vision has become his own. It is principally to them that he owes his profound appreciation of the Christian attitude before the Word of God. He owes them too that vibrant feeling of wonder and adoration before the 'nuptial mystery' and the 'marvellous reciprocation of contraries' realized by the incarnation of the Word. He is indebted to them for that sense of greater universality (in the strictest orthodoxy) because 'it would appear at first that the infinite richness of God contracts and centres in a single point, the humanity of Jesus Christ . . . but this unity reveals itself as capable of integrating everything'.

This rhythm of reflection that combines confidence in received truth with a wide-ranging scope in investigation is also patristic. It is in spontaneous imitation of the Fathers that in him 'the crystal of thought takes fire in the interior and becomes a mystical life'. They have communicated to him their burning love for the Church: for them, as for him, 'the Church is the exact limit of the horizon of Christ's redemption just as, for us, Christ is the horizon of God'. This is why he considers it as futile to stress the many human faults 'which are only too clear to anyone who looks', as it is vital 'to bring to light the admirable secrets of the Church which the world does not know of and which scarcely anyone wishes to recognize'.

The study of the 'Church of the Fathers', in Newman's phrase, has confirmed him in an attitude as distant from 'false tolerance' as it is far from 'confessional narrowness', so that his work, to anyone who wishes to meditate on it, offers a profound ecumenical resonance. One of the great apostles of ecumenism, Patriarch Athenagoras, recognized as much when he sent a messenger to Father Balthasar with a gift of the gold cross of Mount Athos. We may also be glad that as the Faculty of Protestant Theology at Edinburgh University had already done, the Faculty of Catholic Theology at the University of Münster asked him in 1965 to accept an honorary doctorate.

It seems that Balthasar has felt a certain shared situation with that of the Fathers, not in any archaic sense, but in that he too seeks to harness all the features of the culture of his time to make them achieve their full flowering in Christ—though he does not forget, any more than the Fathers did, that all the 'spoils of the Egyptians' are of no use and could, in fact, become a deadly burden if they are not received into a converted heart. For 'it is not the greatest knowledge or the deepest wisdom that is right but the greatest obedience, the deepest humility'; not the sublimity of thought, but the effective simplicity of love.

Effective simplicity are the key-words if we are not to give a fasle idea of where this theologian would wish to lead us: he is theologian only to be apostle. For him, the task of theology, as Albert Beguin has written, 'is to ceaselessly refer back into humble practice the full significance of the revealed word'.

We must confine ourselves here to his written work. As we have already insinuated this work is not narrow or inbred; its 'pauline passion' makes this very clear. Nothing pleases the author more than to wean those his words reach away from dreams, from the illusion of some 'spurious eternity', to immerse

them in the 'true temporality' which is the process of configura-
tion to Christ by submission, *hic et nunc,* to his gospel. This is
shown in one of his latest works, a short treatise with the kierke-
gaardian title: *Wer ist ein Christ?,* which has been translated into
French under the title *Qui est chrétien?*

The other element of his make-up, besides the Fathers, is the
influence of St. Ignatius of Loyola. The need for total commitment to the following of Christ and for fidelity to what one has
received from him, these two great themes of the Spiritual
Exercises were revealed to him by his teacher, Erich Przywara,
in all their force. His own ever deeper study of the *Exercises* has
strengthened this conviction, which he is forever communicating
to others.

Read, for instance, his booklet, published some fifteen years
ago, *Laïcat et plein apostolat;* follow it up with the splendid
chapter he contributed to the symposium *Das Wagnis der
Nachfolge: Zur Theologie des Rätestandes.* One may, if one
wishes, pass over the concrete plans for a secular institute proposed in it; such things are contingent, depending on circumstances of time and place and personal likes and dislikes. But at
this moment, with so many clamouring voices whose Christianity seems marginal arising in the bosom of the Church, those
who are troubled and anxious at the sight of all the spray in the
wash of the great vessel, the Ecumenical Council, even if they
have no stomach for the deeper reaches of his greater works, will
find much comfort in this essay that recalls, so objectively and
precisely, the laws of the gospel. It will also show them what the
true dignity of the layman is, in Christ.

They will also better understand why the Council decided
to include in the dogmatic Constitution on the Church, as
though to contribute to the definition, the two chapters on the
universal call to sanctity and on the externally organized
spiritual life: just as the Old Testament was not confined to
preparing men for the coming of Christ but also had the role
of unfolding, even before the event, the dimensions of his person,
so, and even more so, the Church does not restrict herself to the
instruction of men with a view to the final return of Christ, but
announces that his imprint must be placed on all creation, that
a movement is under way which will end only under new skies
and in a new land. 'She is not only on her way to this event; as

the "mystical parousia" she is its beginning.' And as for those who are determined to be true imitators of Christ in their apostolates, they will find themselves forewarned against the discouragement lying in wait for them when they hear the author say that for these true imitators, 'Christian suffering will not be spared'.

Effective simplicity, we were saying, *of love*. This last is not a word Balthasar pronounces lightly: he feels its full weight. Even before he reckons up the conditions for a Christian to realize it, he sees the human impossibility of it. How could man love man? He would 'perish at the stifling' contact:

> If in the other person nothing is offered but what one already knows fundamentally for oneself—the limitations inherent in his nature, his anguish before them, his constant buffeting by them: death, sickness, folly, chance; a being to whom this anguish can give wings to the most astonishing discoveries— why should the 'I' lose itself for a 'Thou' which the 'I' cannot honestly believe is, at the deepest level, any different from itself? No reason at all, of course! If in my like it is not God I meet; if, in love, no breath of wind brings me the sweet scent of the infinite; if I cannot love my neighbour with any other love than that arising from my finite capacity; if, there-fore, in our meeting, that great reality that bears the name of love does not come from God and return to him—beginning the adventure is not worth the trouble.

> It rescues man neither from his prison nor his solitude. Animals can love one another without knowing God be-cause they have no consciousness of themselves. But as for those beings whose nature permits and forces this reflection, and who have learnt to practise it so profoundly that not only an individual but all humanity can look itself in the face, for them love of another is impossible without God.

But Jesus came and, having promulgated his great command-ment, diffused his Spirit. 'The Fathers of the Church and the medievalists were at considerable pains to explain why his com-ing was so late. We, on the contrary, ask why he did not delay his arrival till today when existence on this planet has become insupportable without him. Be that as it may, the seed he sowed pushes it way above the ground and becomes visible.'

The hour of history has sounded when it has become evident that man cannot be loved except in God—and that God is only loved in 'the sacrament of our brother'. It is also the hour when it must be recognized—Jesus himself was explicit on this subject —that 'all Christian love implies a bursting out of enclosures and inner precincts, an outgoing to the world, to him who does not love, to the lost brother, to the enemy'. The Church is the spouse of Christ but will not be acknowledged as such except in the surpassment that is her love. *Glaubhaft ist nur Liebe.* In all that it is most intimate and pressing, Christian love surpasses 'Christianity' but this very action of surpassing is Christianity itself.[4]

And it is also God himself: '. . . If the supreme reality in God were truth, we should be able to look, with great open eyes, into its abysses, blinded perhaps by so much light, but hampered by nothing in our flight towards truth. But love being the decisive reality, the seraphim cover their faces with their wings, for the mystery of eternal love is such that even the excessive brilliance of its night cannot be glorified except in adoration.'

★

We have barely touched on some of the many themes this immense achievement offers for our consideration, barely indicated some of its characteristics. We must now try to penetrate the secret of this highly personal thought, but whose personality consists solely in a loving search for an objective grasp of the mystery. Our reward (if we are successful) will be a heightened consciousness of the unique originality of our faith and, by that very fact, of every effort of the intelligence which wishes to be faithful to it. Since we cannot fully explore the whole, let us at least point out one of the avenues that leads to its centre.

The precise nature of Balthasar's invitation to us to look on the face of Jesus is conditioned by a rather rigorous interpretation

4. A similar idea will be found in Karl Rahner, 'Is Christianity an Ideology?' in *Concilium*, 1965: 'Unlike an ideology, powerless of its nature to surpass itself, Christianity is, in a sense, more than itself: it is this very movement by which man abandons himself to the mystery at the ground of his being and which ceaselessly escapes him, but which he knows leads on to this mystery, that finds its effective realization in Jesus Christ: a love that draws near and envelops his existence'.

of the christological formula of Chalcedon. The 'density of the human nature' of Christ is altered not a whit by its union to the divinity, no more after the resurrection than during the earthly existence—and the personal unity is not so less perfect that the man Jesus is not the face expressive of God. 'Not for a single instant is the glory of God absent from the Lamb, or the light of the Trinity from that of the incarnate Word.' It follows that for the Christian, negative theology, even when pushed to its extremes, is not detached from its base, the positive theology that illumines that face.

No doubt, for him as for all, the divinity is incomprehensible: *Si comprehenderis, non est Deus.* The dissimilarity between the creator and the creature will always be greater than the similarity. But the situation of the Christian is still not much different from that of the philosopher or any other religious man. He knows that God himself has a face. What appears in Jesus Christ 'is the trinitarian God making himself visible, an object of experience; the face in revelation is not the limit of an infinite without face, it manifests an infinitely determined face'.

In Jesus the believer sees God. For him, therefore, 'what is incomprehensible in God no longer proceeds from a mere ignorance; it is a positive determination by God of the knowledge of faith: the daunting and stupefying incomprehensibility of the fact that God so loved the world that he gave us his only Son, that the God of all plentitude lowered himself not only in his creation but in the conditions of an existence determined by sin, destined for death, removed from God. Such is the obscurity that appears even as it hides itself, the intangible character of God that becomes tangible by the very act of touching him.'

That cannot any longer happen in Christianity what *'cannot but happen'* everywhere else: 'that the finite is, in the last analysis, absorbed by the infinite; the non-identical snuffed out by the identical'; religion devoured by mysticism. Accomplished 'once for all', the humiliation of God in the incarnation cannot be nullified. In the tension manifest in the face of Christ 'between the grandeur of a free God and the abasement of a loving one', is opened before the Christian's eyes 'the heart of the divinity'.

The entire trinitarian teaching and all theology of revelation are bound up with this central vision; they explain one another through it and are themselves necessary for its understanding.

As is normal, while the mind gives its consent to all this by an intuitive impulse, it makes the intelligence alert, satisfies it and finally, like all fruitful thought, poses it more problems than it answers . . .

To finish what we set out to do we shall make another brief incursion, not this time to the core of the doctrine, but to the heart of the spirituality that corresponds to it. (Need we say that our efforts are no substitute for personal reading of his works.) A single word defines this spirituality: it is a spirituality of Holy Saturday.

'. . . There was a day when Nietzsche was right: God was dead, the Word was not heard in the world, the body was interred and the tomb sealed up, the soul descended into the bottomless abyss of sheol.' This descent of Jesus into the kingdom of the dead 'was part of his abasement even if (as St. John admits of the cross) this supreme abasement is already surrounded by the thunderbolts of Easter night. In fact, did not the very descent to hell bring redemption to the souls there?' It prolonged in some manner the cry from the cross: 'Why have you abandoned me?' 'Nobody could ever shout that cry from a deeper abyss than did he whose life was to be perpetually born of the Father.'

But there remains the imitation of Christ. There is a participation, not only sacramental, but contemplative in his mystery. There is an experience of the abandonment on the cross and the descent into hell, an experience of the *poena damni*.[5] There is the crushing feeling of the 'ever greater dissimilarity' of God in the resemblance, however great, between him and the creature; there is the passage through death and darkness, the stepping through 'the sombre door' . . . In conformity to the mission he has received, the prayerful man then experiences the feeling that 'God is dead for him'. And this is a gift of Christian grace— but one receives it unawares. The lived and felt faith, charity, and hope rise above the soul to an inaccessible place, to God. From then on it is 'in nakedness, poverty and humiliation' that the soul cries out to him.[6]

5. Compare the analogous experience described by Pierre Emmanuel in *La face humaine* (Ed. du Seuil, Paris, 1966), pp. 277–8, and which he calls 'the esthetic of Holy Saturday'.
6. See also in *Questions théologiques d'aujourd'hui*, vol. 2, 1965, pp. 280–88: 'Eschatologie'.

Those who have experienced such states[7] afterwards, more often than not, in their humility, see nothing in them but a personal purification. True to his doctrine which refuses to separate charisms and gifts of the Holy Spirit, the ecclesial mission and individual mysticism, Balthasar discerns in it essentially this 'Holy Saturday of contemplation' by which the betrothed, in some chosen few of her members, is made to participate more closely in the redemption wrought by the spouse. We have arrived at a time in history when human consciousness, enlarged and deepened by Christianity, inclines more and more to this interpretation. The sombre experience of Holy Saturday is the price to be paid for the dawn of the new spring of hope, this spring which has been 'canonized in the rose garden of Lisieux': '. . . is it not the beginning of a new creation? The magic of Holy Saturday . . . Deep cave from which the water of life escapes.'

Reading so many passages where this theme is taken up, we discern a distress, a solitude, a night—of the same quality, in fact, as that experienced by 'the Heart of the world'—and we understand that a work that communicates so full a joy must have been conceived in *that* sorrow.

7. Cf. Jules Monchanin, 'Spiritualité du désert' in *Dieu vivant*, 1, 1945, p. 51: 'A naked faith that includes, without knowing it, hope'. Hadewijch, *Mengeldichte,* 16 (Poiron, pp. 127–8), quoted by Jean Orcibal, *Jean de la Croix et les mystiques rhéno-flamands* (1966), p. 108.

7

Holiness in Future

Dear friend,

You ask me what in my opinion will be the characteristic features of holiness in the future. Well, in my opinion, your question cannot be answered. I am no prophet—and I doubt greatly that the prophets themselves could give you an answer.

What new forms will sanctity take in the future? The question goes beyond the scope of forecast or prophecy: prophets never discerned in advance the contingent forms of the great realities they were foretelling. 'Each saint's life is like a new blossoming, an effusion of a miraculous, Eden-like ingenuousness' (Bernanos). Holiness is the work of the Holy Spirit who is not 'this pale, insipid, timeless sun of enlightened reason', who never was and never will be: the Spirit is he who breathes where he will, when he will, as he will. He is liberty, innovation itself, the eternal and intangible innovation of God.

After the event, no doubt, there will be no dearth of explanations. One might enumerate all sorts of reasons, objective or simply ingenious, for the newness of an Augustine, a Francis of Assisi, an Ignatius of Loyola . . . And with a little hindsight, there should not be too much difficulty in showing how this newness was written into the history of Christian cultures, how it shaped them, made them productive, determined their orientation, sometimes for centuries afterwards. Before the event, however, before the budding, who could have described the new blossoming? Who could have foreseen what the individual contribution of an Augustine, a Francis, an Ignatius would be? Similarly, none of us today can seriously venture to sketch, in detail, the portraits of the saints of tomorrow.

On the other hand, it should not be too difficult to indicate certain characteristics which they will *not* have, an exercise which should not be brushed aside as useless. They will not, to begin with, be ideologists. They will not try to define or, to realize in themselves, 'a new type of saint'—any more than a new kind of priest or layman. If they accomplish great things it will not be by dissertations on the courage to dare. If they bring something truly new to the world, if they open up to it fresh perspectives, it will not be by means of wordy generalities on the necessity to create and invent. They will not think to yield to an infantile need for security in attaching themselves to the Church's tradition: this tradition will be a source of strength, not a millstone round their necks.

Perhaps some of them will be reformers who will have to show themselves strict; but none of them will be compulsive critics of what has gone before, their strictness will not be negative, their work of reform will not have a basis of resentment. They will have no time for the facile and erroneous dichotomies set up by men without experience and knowledge of history between the love of God and love of the neighbour, between prayer and action, between the interior life and presence in the world.

They will not confuse the openness of life with the dissolution and disintegration of death, nor the idolatry of man with brotherly charity. They will entertain no pretentions of going one better than the gospel . . . Unlike the cases of some epochs of the 'mystical invasion', the true contemplatives will manage to avoid the cerebral game of 'super-essential and pre-eminent sublimities'; they will learn, if they give themselves the trouble, to construct no less sublime phraseologies in their own field whose simplicity will have nothing in common with those constructions that our present age is tireless in erecting and whose most obvious result is to tear us away from the divine simplicity of the faith and the Christian life. Among them will be found, no doubt, learned and not so learned; but even the most learned and those most spontaneously in tune with all the human progress of their time will entertain no feelings of superiority in their faith, over the believers who have gone before them. As for the less learned, they will be able to say to all who wish to listen, without suffering from any feeling of inferiority, in the words of an early Christian: 'We argue little, but we live'.

A very negative outline, you may well say! But it does not pretend to be anything else. All it is is a negation of some negative traits that had to be disposed of at the beginning to prevent huge errors later on. What then will he be, this saint we are looking forward to? Who, or what, will bring him to us? After what I have just said, do you imagine that I would like to condemn him to being a carbon-copy of the saints of the past? On the contrary! It is because our present epoch is undergoing change more extensive and bewildering that any other before it that the task you have set me appears doubly impossible.

It is not only a question of trying to gauge while the always unpredictable inventions of the Spirit remain an unknown quantity; one has also to speculate on the character and needs of an era beyond one's own. A daring prospect, indeed! What we may be certain of is that the saint of tomorrow will scarcely conform to our ideas, forecasts or desires in his regard. When he appears he may even shock us. He will certainly disconcert us. If God raises him up in our midst we shall be tempted to reject him — unless, as may happen, we pass by and do not see him . . . But he will have his revenge.[1]

I speak of the future, but what I have just said pertains to that part of history that is always beginning again; the part of old, unredeemed man. In his double novelty our saint will also be a man of all times, though in quite a different sense: a doubly new manifestation of that unique new Man who, not being in time, does not repeat the past, but remains a man for all times since, through the vicissitudes of history, he reflects the eternal.[2]

This new man, this saint, so different as he will have to be from his predecessors, will nonetheless reproduce their essential characteristics and it is on these that we may confidently base our predictions. He will be poor, humble, dispossessed. He will have the spirit of the beatitudes. He will neither curse nor flatter; he will love. He will take the gospel at the letter, that is,

1. 'Most people do not understand a saint, ánd even St. Paul and St. John would not seem to be ordinary men. And yet . . .': Newman, *Parochial and Plain Sermons*, 3, 252.

2. Cf. Roger Schutz, *Unanimité dans le pluralisme* (Les Presses de Taizé, 1966): 'What fires us as Christians is the communication of Christ to man. What concerns us most deeply is the advancement of man to God, his spiritual advancement as well as his human . . . But if in our generous openness to man, the signs of other-worldliness disappear from our common vocation, then all we shall be able to show is a special capacity for participation in the contemporary world . . . What we shall not be able to show to men is the event of God, his transcendence, his vertical inrush on the soul . . . A contemplative life that is not integrated is no longer grasped by modern man. But neither is the Christian recognized who allows himself to be wholly absorbed by the human milieu.'

in all its rigour. A hard asceticism will have liberated him from himself. He will be heir to all the faith of Israel but will remember that it has passed through Jesus. He will take up the cross of his saviour and will force himself to follow in the saviour's steps. In his own fashion, something again unforeseeable, he will say to us what a Clement of Alexandria said to the men of *his* time: 'A light has shone in our heaven, brighter than the sun's, softer than our life here below', and it will be a ray of this brightness that he will shed over our night.

Intelligent he will be beyond doubt, the most human of humans, of simple culture perhaps, like a Foucauld, or refined, like a Monchanin. An exceptional human being, he will none-theless be a stimulating example for our mediocre humanity. Fallible like all men but docile to the Spirit, he will share in the discernment promised to the Church and will not be dismayed at even the most radical renewals nor captivated by treacherous novelties. Like so many of his predecessors, by new actions ap-propriate to the new situations, he will be the defender and support of the oppressed. Perhaps, too, he will be a leader of men; perhaps he will be moved, without having wished it, to found a new organization whose daring will, at first, astound all who witness it.

Maybe his will be a role in the public sector of life and *Time* magazine and *Paris Match* and all the other organs of public opinion will have to take note of him. Equally, he may play a lone role, his life lived unnoticed by the mass of ordinary people as by that other 'mass', less numerous than the first but often equally unperceptive and dull, that goes under the name of the 'elite'. It may be that all round him will think him an anachron-ism. His own people may misunderstand, betray or desert him; that simple, human truth of the gospel is also of always. . . . Under forms and on occasions that lie beyond our ken, he will be plunged into the mystery of suffering, into abandonment, into private solitude—into the nausea of sin. In his turn he will be *another Christ*: not, must we repeat, a man desirous of sur-passing Christ but one whose entire life's ideal is to be con-figured to him.

Then, through him as through his master, and in total de-pendence on his master, the face of God—I say so advisedly—will appear.

Numerous voices are raised today to explain to us, with more or less learning, that the time for 'ontology' is past; that our belief in a heavenly Father is only a mythical projection; that all our theology should be relegated to the back of the book-shelves or done away with altogether to make way for man. The philosophers who treated of God belonged, it goes without saying, to the world's infancy! But now, of course, we have reached adulthood (since yesterday!) and we ought, with all speed, discard the remnants of primitive thought that still cling to us!

It is explained to us (yet again!) that there is no truth but the 'verifiable', no evidence but the empirical; that the images of Scripture are hiding no reality; that scientific man has bade goodbye to religious man; that our faith is puerile—some make no bones about it and say it is 'infantile'—our hope illusory, Christian charity which we proclaim, an unhealthy exaggeration . . . Submitted daily to this sort of thing, the believer allows himself to be disturbed. Some despair, while others, for a time at least, beguiled by the new myths, close their eyes and take the road to a new capivity in Babylon. It is not always easy to resist such a solid front, to distinguish the true from the false, to see the point where abuse begins, to catch out criticism in its barefaced caricatures—and matters are made no easier by the apparently reasonable forms a spiritual blindness may take!

But let a saint come on the scene . . . and the miracle happens again. 'These times', the Abbé Monchanin confided, 'people have said that they sense God through me . . .' So it was yesterday—and so it will be tomorrow.[3] The veil is suddenly rent. The vista of eternity opens. The night becomes luminous. Formidable criticisms soon appear ridiculous. In the face of such plenitude—of such love—of such joy, everything yields. All negations cancel out before the indisputable Presence. Man breathes again. Of a sudden he senses, before analysing it—and even afterwards it may defy analysis—the religious mediocrity that made him vulnerable to chimerical criticisms, that caused his illness. When a saint passes, it is a call to conversion.

We may expect that this great saint we long for, which 'our age so badly needs', will be a man who walks 'a free and untrodden path, driven by the fullness of the religious vigour of

3. Cf. Teilhard de Chardin: 'to give to God . . . as the saints did . . . a truly real value'.

his time'; unifying and purifying them in himself he will draw the many aimless searchings and wasted energies of his contemporaries to God; for an entire generation he will thus become a clarion call and a leader, a living symbol at that Christian renewal to which all are invited. Such a man it is that we await, and which of us would wish for anyone else?

But do we not sometimes dream of a saint who, at a blow, would transform our social structures? Or a saint who, by some miracle, would initiate that fraternal society or, at least, lay its foundations? Or a saint who would be acknowledged as such, without gross deformation, by public opinion? Or a saint who, cutting through the knot of our contradictions, would lighten our task as men? Perhaps we have even imagined a new kind of sanctity which would not take root in that same soil of sacrifice and would not participate in that destiny as He whose disciples all the saints before now have wished to be? A saint who would not be a sign of contradiction?

If we have thought so, let us reread the gospel and drive out all dreams and forecasts, let us once more take up our modest task as men, and have confidence in God: the race of saints is not at all a disappearing one.